THE LAST POLAR BEAR

FACING THE TRUTH OF A WARMING WORLD

A PHOTOGRAPHIC JOURNEY
BY STEVEN KAZLOWSKI

Theodore Roosevelt IV • Charles Wohlforth • Daniel Glick • Richard Nelson • Nick Jans • Frances Beinecke

Made possible in part through the generosity of
Campion Foundation

With additional support from Carolyn Moore and the George L. Shields Foundation, Ann and Ron Holz, Chris and Mary Troth, Hugh & Jane Ferguson Foundation, and Ellen Ferguson

BRAIDED RIVER, SEATTLE

Contents

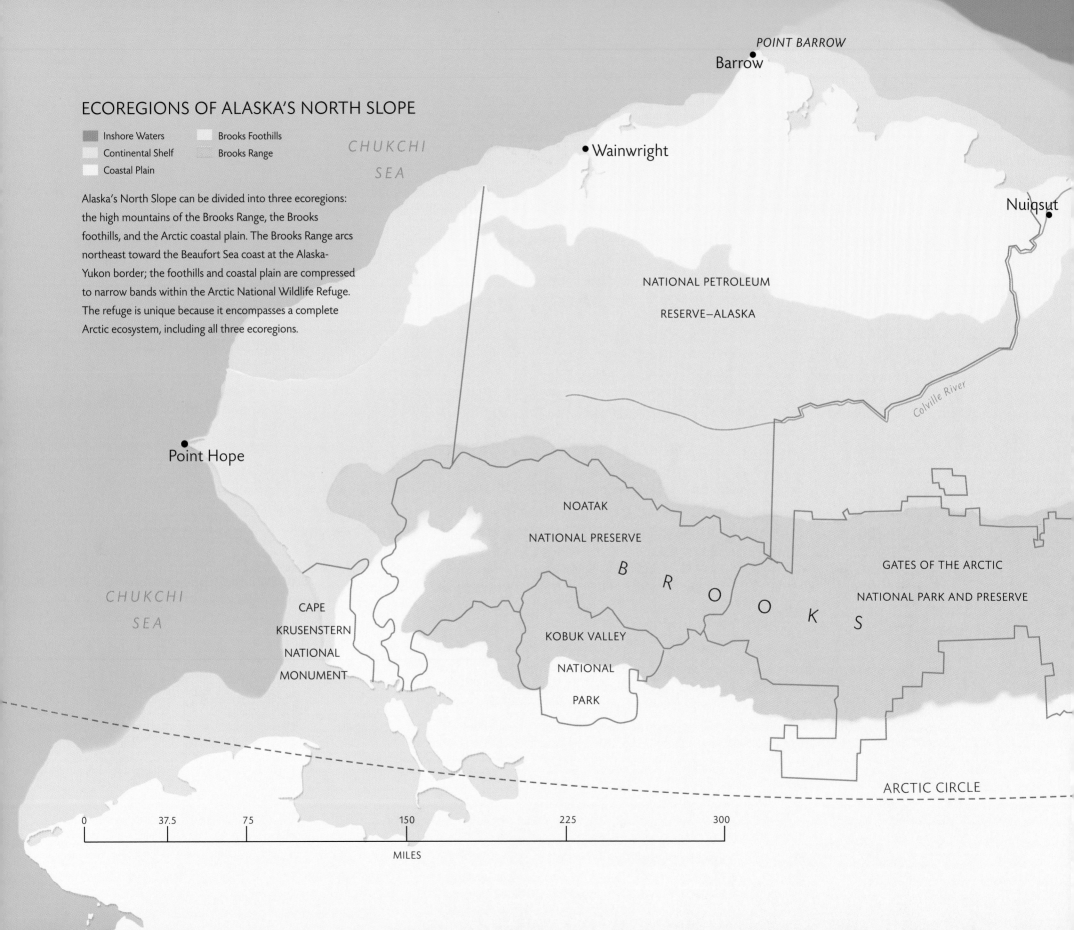

ECOREGIONS OF ALASKA'S NORTH SLOPE

- Inshore Waters
- Continental Shelf
- Coastal Plain
- Brooks Foothills
- Brooks Range

Alaska's North Slope can be divided into three ecoregions: the high mountains of the Brooks Range, the Brooks foothills, and the Arctic coastal plain. The Brooks Range arcs northeast toward the Beaufort Sea coast at the Alaska-Yukon border; the foothills and coastal plain are compressed to narrow bands within the Arctic National Wildlife Refuge. The refuge is unique because it encompasses a complete Arctic ecosystem, including all three ecoregions.

CHUKCHI SEA

POINT BARROW

Barrow

Wainwright

Nuiqsut

NATIONAL PETROLEUM

RESERVE—ALASKA

Colville River

Point Hope

CHUKCHI SEA

NOATAK

NATIONAL PRESERVE

B R O O K S

GATES OF THE ARCTIC

NATIONAL PARK AND PRESERVE

CAPE KRUSENSTERN NATIONAL MONUMENT

KOBUK VALLEY NATIONAL PARK

ARCTIC CIRCLE

0   37.5   75   150   225   300

MILES

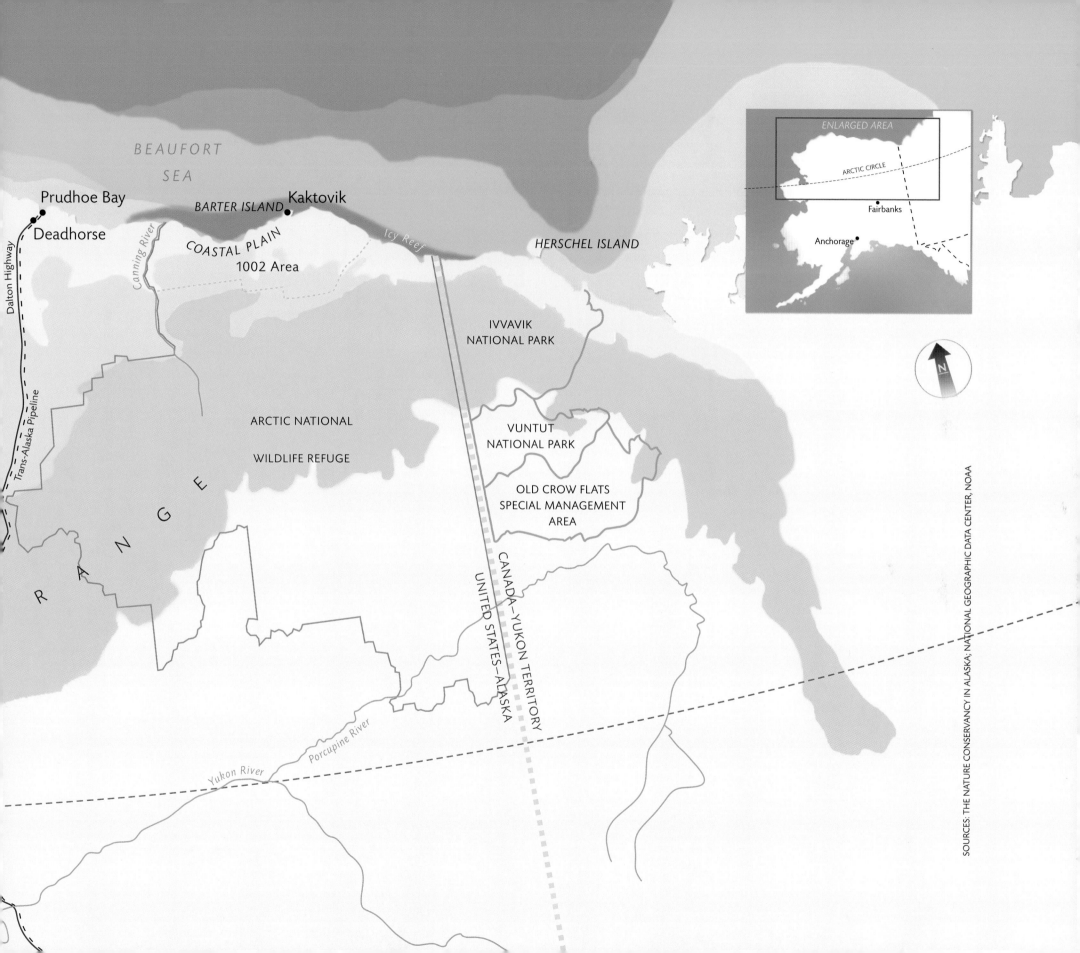

BEAUFORT
SEA

Prudhoe Bay

Deadhorse

BARTER ISLAND   Kaktovik

COASTAL PLAIN

1002 Area

Canning River

Icy Reef

HERSCHEL ISLAND

Dalton Highway

Trans-Alaska Pipeline

R A N G E

ARCTIC NATIONAL

WILDLIFE REFUGE

IVVAVIK
NATIONAL PARK

VUNTUT
NATIONAL PARK

OLD CROW FLATS
SPECIAL MANAGEMENT
AREA

CANADA–YUKON TERRITORY
UNITED STATES–ALASKA

Porcupine River

Yukon River

N

ENLARGED AREA

ARCTIC CIRCLE

Fairbanks

Anchorage

SOURCES: THE NATURE CONSERVANCY IN ALASKA; NATIONAL GEOGRAPHIC DATA CENTER, NOAA

ABOVE *A polar bear sow and her cubs on the tundra (coastal area, Arctic National Wildlife Refuge)*

LEFT *Frozen seascape of pressure ridges in the pack ice (Chukchi Sea, near Barrow, Alaska)*

Helen Cherullo

PREFACE

PHOTOGRAPHER STEVEN KAZLOWSKI'S PORTFOLIO of oversize glossy images meld the polar bear and the consequences of the melting Arctic ice into the compelling story you see in this book. He has gone literally to the ends of the world, in unimaginable weather, to capture photographs of polar bears and their Arctic world that few are able duplicate. From a polar bear mother emerging from her den with brand-new cubs to extremely shy ringed seals hauled out on the ice to a polar bear traveling with its elusive companion the Arctic fox, the images in this book are truly amazing, and hard won.

Flipping through these photographs in rapid succession, Steve had a story to tell about the plight of the polar bear and the threats to its Arctic habitat. Together, he and I traveled to Washington DC in the spring of 2007 during the Climate Crisis Rally to take his story to congressional offices, from Washington State's representatives and senators to those of Alaska.

Dropping in at the offices of elected representatives is a heady reminder of the power of the democratic process, that we are a government of the people. As such, Steve and I were received and listened to with patience and a respectful sense of duty. At each office we visited, we were met with this same question:

"What is it that you want us to do?" The question was a mix of wariness and concern. The people we met with were practiced, formal, and polite, but most were stirred by those photographs they saw.

The last of Steve's images showed a polar bear in a zoo. "If we do nothing as a society, and the ice continues to melt," Steve said, "within decades, this could be the only place on earth a polar bear will be found."

LEFT *A polar bear's big, flat front paws work like paddles to push water as it swims (Anchorage Zoo, Anchorage, Alaska). If we do nothing as a society, and the ice continues to melt, zoos could be the only place on earth where polars bears can be found.*

The pronouncement stirred a memory in me of being very young—five years old or so—and spending hot summers outside Chicago in the late 1950s at Brookfield Zoo. The animals I dearly loved were the giraffes and the elephants—and the polar bears. My hands became sticky from the July heat and from feeding all of them marshmallows. The beautiful, rounded white bears and the plump, white sweet treats I carefully tossed to them seemed a perfect match.

At that young age, I understood that wild animals came from wild places that were far away—most of them countries beginning with the letter "A." Africa, Australia, Antarctica—the Arctic. When I saw them living in their concrete partitions in the heat of this Midwest suburb, any connection to their natural environment or their native food source was invisible to me. They loved marshmallows and sunshine, just like me.

Very little is definitely known about the polar bear. The polar bear has not been studied as extensively as other large mammals, in large part because its habitat is so remote and harsh. When Steve wanted to capture an image of a mother with her cubs, it was a months-long ordeal, capped off by a month of waiting in subzero agony, not even sure the animals were still alive or in their den.

Scientists who study polar bear populations do so in parts of the Arctic with distinct enough ecologies that the result is differing observations of the world's dozen or so known polar bear populations. Among polar bear biologists, there may not be right or wrong answers, only different observations. We chose scientific advisers Steven Amstrup and his colleague Geoffrey York—United States Geological Service biologists studying the Alaskan polar bear—to review *The Last Polar Bear* because Steve Kazlowski's photographs in this book are predominantly from Alaska, in the far northern Beaufort and Chukchi seas. Findings by scientists working in other countries may differ. This book also includes invaluable observations and stories from the indigenous Iñupiat who know polar bears intimately from living among them for centuries.

The heart of the issue of the polar bear's continued survival in the wild is not in dispute, however. Adaptations critical to the survival of a species have allowed them to thrive in the remote and inhospitable northern region of the globe for thousands of years. As the ice melts, they literally have no place else to move to—zoos notwithstanding.

The polar bear has put a face to climate change for those of us far from the Arctic. The plight of the white bear is among the first stories to shock the public and bring voice to the science that has to date failed to move us. The scientific community has determined that there is irrefutable proof that the decline in numbers and health of the polar bear is due to ice melting. Their food source—dependent on polar sea ice and ice floes remaining close to the continental shelf that supports an intact food chain—is threatened. To make matters worse, climate change has impacted the Arctic more than any other place on the planet, even more than the Antarctic. Arctic ice is much thinner because under it is the Arctic Ocean, which absorbs heat and accelerates melting of the polar ice cap, whereas under the Antarctic ice is land—a continent.

The changes to the polar bear's habitat are caused by climate change, and carbon emissions from human activity are a significant cause. At last, through the story of the polar bear, the consequences of letting this human activity go unchecked have struck an emotional chord. Through this book and the resulting public presentations and traveling museum exhibit, we hope to make a bridge to the place where people begin to take action. It is clear that habitats will change—not only for the polar bear, but for all of us—and there will be worldwide consequences. Like the polar bear, humans have also evolved to complement their current surroundings. Changes will be formidable. Rising sea levels, desertification, increases in disease, and consequences to food sources and pollination certainly involve difficulties to overcome, contend with, and adapt to. Some will be insurmountable. Even greater sacrifices will be necessary if nothing is done right now.

The polar bear's story is ultimately our story.

Either by legislation or by being listed as an endangered species—and by the will of the people—the polar bear is the one concrete element that may lead businesses and the markets, individuals and politicians, governments and those that love to hang on to the security of the status quo to places they have been loath to go. Carbon emissions will need to be controlled on a worldwide basis to safeguard the natural systems on the planet to ensure it remains hospitable to life as we know it. It will take courage and leadership, innovation and investment. And it will require change.

This is what Steve and I asked of our elected representatives when we visited Washington DC early in 2007: to learn, to care, to show leadership, and to act.

Sometimes the weight of the evidence against the continued survival of the polar bear is overwhelming, and it can be hard to remain hopeful. Steve and the eloquent essayists in this book are haunted by an unacceptable thought: witnessing the last polar bear within our lifetime.

But if enough of us learn, care, and act, the pressure we can bring to bear on our elected representatives will lead to change. This book offers solid scientific reporting to help us learn the what and why of climate change; evocative photographs to connect our caring nature to the plight of the Arctic; and concrete, doable actions that each of us can take, right now, to help reverse the consequences of climate change. Together, we can forge a positive future for the polar bear—and for all of us.

Helen Cherullo is publisher of The Mountaineers Books and executive director of Braided River Books, a not-for-profit conservation division of The Mountaineers Books. The Last Polar Bear is the first book for the new imprint, built on the legacy of books and extensive public outreach on behalf of the Arctic National Wildlife Refuge, Yellowstone to Yukon Conservation Initiative, and wild places of western North America. For more information visit www.BraidedRiverBooks.org.

RIGHT *Cows, calves, and juvenile walruses crowd on an ice floe (confluence of the Beaufort and Chukchi seas).*

ABOVE *King eiders and common eiders rarely fly together in large flocks (spring migration, Arctic coast, near Barrow).*

ABOVE *The polar bear's black skin can be seen beneath its wet fur (Arctic Ocean, Arctic National Wildlife Refuge).*

Steven Kazlowski

Open leads of water along the Alaskan Arctic coast traditionally have been lined with broken jumbles of saltwater ice, rough pieces and boulders up to two stories high forming pressure ridges almost impossible to traverse. These pressure ridges are mixed with flat pans of multiyear ice, created over time by winds, currents, and cold temperatures. On a cloudy day, you can look out across the horizon to the north where overcast skies meet the uneven rumple of ice, seeing ominous-looking black clouds that indicate open water in the distance.

In this cold place, the winds and currents can literally change the landscape before your eyes. In no time at all, the ice can crumble beneath your feet or push up into mountains; it can break off with little or no warning and take you away with it. On the surface, the white Arctic coastal environment appears to be still and benign, but it is constantly moving and innately dangerous.

This is what the edge of the ice at the top of the world is like: a living thing that opens and closes. Traditionally in late autumn, when the ice closes, there is less open water. And then springtime arrives and the ice opens up, with more open water drawing an incredible array of life to this marine yet terrestrial environment, from beluga and bowhead whales to walruses and bearded and ringed seals, polar bears, and Arctic foxes. You can sit on the edge of an open lead and, over the course of a very special spring day, watch thousands of migrating birds winging northeast, flying low along the edge of the ice. Then pods of belugas may arrive, their immense bodies rolling through the water. The frozen landscape is vacant one moment, and in the next, species too numerous to count appear out of nowhere.

In the midst of it all, the great white bear, *nanuq*, walks up and down the leads and on the moving pack ice, looking for seals while followed by its companion the Arctic fox. The bears themselves almost look like part of the ice at times, their white coats sometimes transparent.

The ice, the open water, and the continental shelf below all create the foundation for an incredible web of life. Whales instinctively know how to swim from lead to lead, feeding off the arthropods of their rich food chain. The whales wait for just the right conditions so they can move northeast along the coast into their summer feeding grounds. They travel under the ice some of the time, with the leads freezing and closing behind them and opening before them, and somehow they know how to gauge the living edge of the ice, moving within the opening channels of water. The edge of the ice is like an oasis in the desert—a solitary place abundant with the necessities of life—and every animal around comes by it to feed and migrate through.

When I decided to become a wildlife photographer, I found both the solitude and the wildlife I was looking for in the Alaskan Arctic along the Dalton Highway, known locally as the Haul Road. This unpaved road created for oil development also allows access to this extraordinary place for other purposes—such as wilderness exploration and photography in remote places, a seeming paradox. What occurs far away from this sparsely populated place—the oil-consuming acts of millions of people, which contribute to climate change—are destroying this rare and wild habitat, and this kind of destruction very likely will occur across the globe if those countless actions go unchecked.

How I ended up working on this book project is almost as intriguing as the polar bears themselves. During my early years in the Arctic, although I saw many coastal animals—grizzly bears, musk ox, Arctic foxes—I never encountered a polar bear. I never planned to photograph polar bears in Alaska at all, yet as of this writing I have captured images of polar bears in their natural habitat for more than eight years.

LEFT *Ringed seals on multiyear ice don't stray far from an exit hole, this one under water (20 miles offshore, Point Barrow, Alaska).*

ABOVE *A beluga whale during spring migration, when whales swim from lead to lead (Chukchi Sea, near Point Barrow, Alaska). Leads, which are often long and narrow, may extend for many miles.*

CLOCKWISE FROM TOP LEFT
Walruses rear their calves for two years in the rich environment over the continental shelf (spring, Bering Sea). / Bowhead whales in a lead, a narrow opening in the ice where open water lets them surface to breathe (Chukchi Sea, near Point Barrow, Alaska). / A spotted seal pup / A watchful bearded seal and her pup (spring, Bering Sea)

My first spring photographing on the Haul Road, I got my initial taste of Arctic weather. One morning as I was trudging through deep snow in bone-chilling cold to photograph a herd of musk ox, I realized that my skin felt as if it were on fire. Although I was wearing several layers of warm clothing, my exposed skin was burning from the severe cold. I didn't understand how these animals, let alone the people who live here, could withstand such conditions. As the musk ox stood within their ring of trampled snow on a frozen river, with no tracks outside the circle's perimeter, I could tell they hadn't moved in weeks. It was the start of their calving season and one calf had already dropped, yet they stayed where they were, conserving their energy.

There is an eerie silence to this place at times, and at others the wind sounds as though the skin of the earth is being peeled off. You have to find comfort in being uncomfortable in order to push through it and see the kind of peace offered by this often rough, weathered environment. That year, spring became new to me, drawing my attention.

The Haul Road ends in Deadhorse, at Prudhoe Bay, and it was there I met Bill Morris, who was working on the North Slope for Alaska Telecom. He encouraged me to travel to Kaktovik, a small Iñupiaq Eskimo village along the eastern Alaskan Arctic coast. Initially I wasn't interested, but Bill's stories of the place soon changed my mind. I flew to the village of some three hundred residents and set up camp in an Alaska Telecom hut, courtesy of Bill. The freezer-like container on stilts had no windows or furniture and was filled with computers, all topped off by a 100-foot antenna. But there was enough room to roll out my sleeping bag on the floor, and the hut had one very attractive feature: ample heat. I spent three weeks there. On my first night in town, the village's public safety officer, whom I had met on the plane from Deadhorse, gave me a ride out to a whale-bone pile, where I saw my first polar bear.

Before long, I met some of the local folks, including bush pilot

Walt Audi, his partner, Merylin Traynor, and Ed Traynor, all who operate the Waldo Arms Hotel. I ended up staying with them while doing odd jobs and washing dishes to earn my keep. But I began to go looking for polar bears, borrowing Ed's recently purchased used Subaru, which smelled like rotten whale meat and didn't start reliably. I had seen only one polar bear since arriving and was about to give up when another bear finally materialized, and I started getting pictures. Then a villager named Fred Kaleak invited me to hang out at the whale-bone pile at night with him, his family, and some friends. It was a great opportunity to get to know some of the people in the village.

Whaling has been a primary means of acquiring food for Native people in the Arctic for thousands of years, and it has been officially recognized as a traditional part of their subsistence way of life. After a successful hunt, the whalers strip the whale carcass of its meat and other usable parts, leaving its bones and scraps, which the bears make good use of in the fall as they wait for the ocean to freeze up so they can hunt ringed seals.

It was amazing, at one point seeing all these seagoing bears swimming up like crocodiles from every direction and then emerging from the water as huge, lumbering land animals. They would feed, play, and curiously check me out. At the end of the fall season, as the ocean froze over, it was time for them to move on. By then, I was hooked on polar bears—who they are, what they do, where they go.

My growing interest in polar bears led me to explore the rest of the Arctic coast of Alaska, from farther east to the far west. To learn

CLOCKWISE FROM TOP LEFT
Two barren-ground caribou along the unpaved Dalton Highway, also known as the Haul Road; created for oil development, it also provides access for wilderness exploration in the remote Arctic (spring, North Slope of the Brooks Range). / A musk ox bull, cow, and calf amid their herd, which might stay in one spot for weeks during calving season, despite excruciating cold (Haul Road, north of the Brooks Range) / Photographer Steven Kazlowski on the frozen Chukchi Sea / Swimming polar bear sow and cubs look like crocodiles (Barter Island, Arctic National Wildlife Refuge).

about the ice and get around on it, I needed to learn from the people who have for generations spent their lives on the ice, so in spite of my innate shyness, I was compelled to introduce myself to them. To my surprise and continuing gratitude, they eventually welcomed me into their communities.

I learned many things from my friends in the Arctic. The indigenous people in this book are the Iñupiat; one person is an Iñupiaq, which is also the name of their language. In the fall, those who inhabit the eastern Alaskan Arctic hunt for seals and bowhead whales from boats along the edge of the ice and in large areas of open water as well as along the coast using snow machines. In the eastern Arctic, they also hunt caribou in fall and winter. In the western and central Arctic, ties to the ocean and hunting on the ice are strong, but getting out on the ice to open water is difficult—you have to cross rough pressure ridges. In these areas, where the Iñupiat have whaled on spring ice for thousands of years, they work together as a community, using axes and shovels to break trail, making highways across the ice to the open water.

My new friends generously allowed me to go hunting with them, traveling by snowmobiles, towing sleds and aluminum or skin boats, and setting up gypsy camps out on the ice and along the coast. Their shelters are often tied-down wall tents made with floors of Styrofoam and plywood, with caribou, brown bear, and polar bear skins laid down for warmth beneath sleeping bags.

The hunters taught me how to live in temperatures of minus 50 degrees Fahrenheit. And I learned how to use the drifting snow as a compass: in parts of that country, the wind blows in a certain direction most of the time, so you always know which way is east and west, north and south.

LEFT *A young polar bear (coastal plain, Arctic National Wildlife Refuge)*
RIGHT *Merylin Traynor and bush pilot Walt Audi operate the Waldo Arms Hotel (Kaktovik, Alaska).*

Two large boars stranded on a beach wait for freeze-up (autumn, coastal plain, Arctic National Wildlife Refuge).

CLOCKWISE FROM TOP LEFT
Polar bears congregate at a whale carcass left after a successful Iñupiaq autumn whale hunt (coastal plain, Arctic National Wildlife Refuge). / A polar bear family at bowhead whale vertebrae (coastal plain, Arctic National Wildlife Refuge) / A mother polar bear with two cubs (autumn, coastal plain, Arctic National Wildlife Refuge) / Autumn, coastal plain, Arctic National Wildlife Refuge

ABOVE *Two sows and a subadult at play on the pack ice*
(autumn, coastal plain, Arctic National Wildlife Refuge)

Pure white polar bear fur reflects
the color of light around it, so at sunrise
and sunset bears can look yellow-orange,
and in clouds and fog they appear blue.
In the late winter and spring, oils from killed
prey and other stains can give a
polar bear a creamy color.

ABOVE *At play. A polar bear's long, glossy outer hairs easily shed water, while the dense, wooly underfur provides warmth (autumn, coastal plain, Arctic National Wildlife Refuge).*

RIGHT *A polar bear rolls in the autumn snow to cool off (coastal plain, Arctic National Wildlife Refuge).*

The Iñupiat are strong people. They love their country; they love that ecosystem—an environment that seemed, when I first arrived, too hard to live in and survive, never mind enjoy.

Back in the late 1980s I was very interested in the problem of global warming. After obtaining my degree in marine biology, I worked in the Florida Keys for a year, assisting on a study to determine the cause of coral bleaching. My early research would come full circle and combine with my wildlife photography to shape the concept of this book: how climate change is affecting the Arctic, and polar bears in particular.

In the far north, the ice conditions are changing, affecting not only polar bears but all creatures that are sustained by a relationship with the Arctic ice. The Iñupiat talk about the sea ice being half as thick as it used to be, and they say there is far more open water in the middle of winter than when they were young. One Iñupiaq elder, Clyde Ahmaogak, remembers when the sea ice at Barrow used to be within a couple miles of land during the summer. Today the ice has been measured at 100 or more miles from shore. Now there is less and less multiyear ice with the giant boulders and glacier icebergs, as found in the past. In Barrow this year, it was mostly new ice. And although scientists are far from understanding all the implications of these changes, the people who live in the midst of this shifting landscape are already wondering what the future might hold.

The contributors' essays within these pages offer a crucial link between polar bears, people, and many other animals, their melting habitat, and climate change. Ted Roosevelt introduces the complex political landscape affecting the Arctic. Charles Wohlforth traces the polar bear's path toward being listed as a threatened species. Daniel Glick offers a primer on global climate change that illuminates the intricacy of our planet's health. Richard Nelson ruminates on the ages-old relationship between the Arctic's two ingenious predators: Iñupiaq hunters and the polar bear. Nick Jans shows us the

conundrums an oil-dependent world presents to the Arctic. Frances Beinecke of the Natural Resources Defense Council urges us to make changes not only for the polar bear's sake but for our own as well. An interview with Arnold Brower Sr. provides the perspective of an Iñupiaq elder on the importance of the subsistence way of life for his people. And along with excerpts from my journal, I offer these images as witness to an iconic species and an ecosystem that could be lost to future generations if we, as a global community, do not take action now.

Photographer **Steven Kazlowski** *earned a degree in marine biology from Towson State University in Baltimore before setting out for Alaska to pursue his true passion: wildlife photography. His photos have been featured in* TIME, National Wildlife, Audubon, Backpacker, Canadian Geographic, *and* National Geographic for Kids *magazines, and he has produced photographs for three books:* Alaska's Bears of the North, Alaska's Wildlife of the North, *and* Alaska Wildlife Impressions. *Kazlowski is known within the photography community for his skills of observation and his determination to capture an image even in extreme weather conditions. He produces and distributes his own postcards and other print photographs via his website,* www.lefteyepro.com. *He spends most of the year in Alaska, waiting and watching for the perfect photograph.*

RIGHT *Snoozing on late-summer ice (Arctic Ocean, near the Arctic National Wildlife Refuge)*

ABOVE *Iñupiaq whaler Price Brower, wearing polar bear mittens, watches a flat pan of ice move rapidly through an open lead, a potentially dangerous condition for whalers (springtime, Chukchi Sea, near Barrow). Arctic ice is always opening and closing; in summer it's gone, then in fall it freezes up again.*

ABOVE *Iñupiaq whalers in an* umiak, *a traditional hunting boat made of bearded seal–skins, return to their camp on the edge of a lead (springtime, Chukchi Sea, near Barrow).*

Over the last two decades, scientists have learned substantially more about climate change and the threat it poses to the world's biodiversity.

Theodore Roosevelt IV

Arctic Canary: Why the White Bear Matters

SEVERAL YEARS AGO, WHEN I ATTENDED a meeting of the governing council of the Wilderness Society held in Denali National Park, Alaska, I was able to justify a much-desired trip to the Arctic National Wildlife Refuge as well. I had long been concerned about Congress opening the coastal plain of the refuge to oil drilling— I worried about the potential impact this would have on the Porcupine caribou herd's calving grounds and on the female polar bears that use parts the coastal plain of Alaska's North Slope, including areas of the Arctic Refuge, for birthing dens.

One afternoon, just after a stunningly beautiful Denali had emerged from the clouds for the first time since our arrival, I left my Wilderness Society colleagues and attempted to fly to Prudhoe Bay via Fairbanks. Imagining that the glorious sight of Denali was a good omen, I assumed it would be easy to fly across the Brooks Range. Alaskan weather had other plans, though, and I was grounded for a day and a half in Fairbanks. When the weather finally relented, I got as far as Prudhoe Bay, where I met the legendary bush pilot Walt Audi. Since I had arrived almost two days later than expected, Walt could take me only part of the way to the Arctic Refuge, leaving me in the town of Kaktovik while he handled other customers.

Frustrated by yet another delay, I decided to look around the small town and discovered some hauntingly beautiful photographs of Alaskan wildlife at the town's hotel. A modest man approached me and wanted to know what I thought of the photographs. They were stunning, I replied, and asked if he knew where I could buy a few. This is how I met this book's photographer, Steven Kazlowski. Steve and I became friends, and I consequently learned more about the impact of global climate change on polar bears.

Recent observations reveal that, with the Arctic ice sheet melting earlier in the spring and returning later in the fall, polar bears are now forced to spend more time on land than usual. Unable to hunt their traditional prey—the ringed seal—polar bears are being found with greater frequency around garbage dumps and human habitations, increasing the possibility of conflict with humans.

At first, one might think that a warming Arctic would not pose a particularly serious threat to polar bears. Wouldn't a warmer Arctic be a more benign habitat? The reality is just the reverse, though, and observations of female polar bears illustrate why.

Late each autumn, pregnant polar bears look for dens in which to birth and nurse one, two, or (fairly rarely) three cubs. The cubs are born blind, toothless, virtually helpless, weighing little more than a pound. The next March or April, the cubs emerge from the den weighing 15 to 25 pounds, following their mother, who has lost up to two-thirds of her weight. The ravenous mother needs to regain the weight she lost raising her cubs. But time is against her.

Summer is not a time of plenty for polar bears, as it is for many other animals. With the approach of summer, the ice begins to melt, and a polar bear's ability to find seals on that ice dwindles and finally ceases until the winter ice returns. For the mother bear, this situation is particularly acute: whereas the rest of the population—males and nonpregnant females—have spent the winter hunting and maintaining fat reserves for the leaner summer months, the mother bear has been fasting in her den, birthing and nursing her cubs.

Despite this vulnerable period after emerging from the den, the mother polar bear is incredibly well adapted to her harsh Arctic habitat, so much so that if her environment becomes more benign, her survival may be threatened. Polar bears have a layer of fat up to 4.3 inches thick that provides insulation. Their guard hair is hollow, providing more insulation, and is water-repellent, adding to their

LEFT *Barren-ground caribou of the Porcupine herd on their calving grounds (coastal plain, Arctic National Wildlife Refuge)*

ABOVE *A male guards his meal of a bowhead whale carcass, at sunrise (coastal plain, Arctic National Wildlife Refuge).*

LEFT *Ringed seals, a favorite prey of polar bears, are very wary—difficult to photograph under the best of conditions (springtime, Chukchi Sea).*

RIGHT *The village of Kaktovik, Alaska, population about 280 (springtime, Brooks Range in the distance)*

buoyancy. Underneath their white fur is black skin that can absorb heat from the Arctic sun. Their large, furry feet act as snowshoes and make them strong swimmers. Indeed, polar bears spend so much of their time on the polar ice cap, hunting, sleeping, mating, and swimming across nonfrozen areas of the ocean, that many scientists consider them to be a marine mammal rather than a terrestrial one. Polar bears have a longer neck than their close cousin the brown bear (*Ursus arctos*), enabling them to raise their head out of the water for a better view. They may have keener eyesight and hearing than the brown bear. Polar bears' sense of smell is so good that they can sniff out a carcass up to a distance of 20 miles away.

Many scientists consider the male polar bear, which can be more than twice the size of a female, to be the world's largest nonaquatic carnivore. It is certainly bigger than the inland grizzly or brown bear found in Yellowstone National Park and elsewhere, but it may be rivaled by the Kodiak bear (*Ursus arctos middendorffi*), a subspecies of brown bear that feasts on a particularly rich diet of salmon (which accounts for its large size). Both the Kodiak and the polar bear are enormous, and exceptionally large males may exceed 1,700 pounds. Situated at the top of the food chain in the Arctic, polar bears each require a huge territory, ranging from 70,000 to as much as 100,000 square miles. As a result, the world's population of polar bears is relatively small, estimated at 21,500 to 25,000.

Although well adapted to her environment, the mother bear has a formidable task when she emerges from her den with her cubs. Not only must she find food to replenish herself, but she must school her cubs. She teaches them to swim, a skill they develop quickly. Once they learn to swim, they eagerly jump off ice floes, seemingly for the sheer pleasure of it—though the young bears often are unable to climb back on the floe and instead rely on their mother to pull them out numerous times. She also defends her cubs against approaching males, which can kill cubs in an effort to then breed with the female, though a male's size alone makes a prudent mother bear uneasy.

LEFT *Male polar bear in an autumn snowstorm (coastal plain, Arctic National Wildlife Refuge)*

RIGHT *A polar bear den, dug from a snowdrift, is decorated with claw marks around its entrance hole (early spring, Arctic coast, west of Arctic National Wildlife Refuge).*

Most importantly, she teaches her cubs how to hunt. During their first year, the mother bear must spend so much of her time looking out for her cubs that her hunting time is reduced; whenever possible, she will feed on leftover prey killed by another bear. During the second year, when the cubs are bigger and stronger, they become good hunters in their own right. At that point, the mother bear and her cubs face few serious threats, other than humans and adult male polar bears or the rare case of being impaled by a walrus defending itself.

Fifty years ago, the greatest threat to polar bears was indiscriminate hunting. Bears were shot by tourists from icebreakers and by soldiers based in the Arctic. Some trophy hunters even used airplanes. Public outrage over unsporting hunting techniques, coupled with the species' dwindling numbers, brought considerable popular opposition to hunting the polar bear in the countries bordering the Arctic. With the passage of the Marine Mammal Protection Act of 1972, the United States banned the hunting of polar bears except by Native peoples. The following year, in November 1973, the Soviet Union, Canada, Norway, Denmark (of which Greenland is a part), and the United States entered into a treaty—the International Agreement on the Conservation of Polar Bears and Their Habitat—to protect these threatened animals. The treaty was signed during the cold war at a time when there was little cooperation between the Soviet Union and the United States. While not perfect, the agreement has resulted in restrictions on hunting, helped create protected areas, and furthered the exchange of scientific research. This last outcome has been particularly important because the polar bear's habitat and range covers five countries; it is only through this international cooperation that a more complete understanding of polar bears has begun to emerge.

Today, polar bears face a far more serious threat in the form of climate change. The warming of their natural environment has a profoundly negative impact on their highly successful form of hunting, which has developed over millennia in the frozen Arctic. For example, in the southern part of polar bears' range—southwestern Hudson Bay near the town of Churchill, Manitoba—the bears' hunting season has

LEFT *Roaming the coastal plain (autumn, Arctic National Wildlife Refuge, Brooks Range in the distance)*

ESTIMATED POLAR BEAR POPULATIONS AND RANGES

SOURCE: INTERNATIONAL UNION FOR CONSERVATION OF NATURE AND NATURAL RESOURCES/SPECIES SURVIVAL COMMISION, POLAR BEAR SPECIALIST GROUP, 2006

Figure 1. Estimated polar bear populations throughout the five countries with Arctic land are very rough, depending on current research status. Polar bears are little studied in Russia and East Greenland, whereas Canada's polar bear populations have been extensively mapped.

decreased significantly because the ice melts sooner in the spring and freezes later in the fall. Farther north, polar bears encounter more open water, requiring them to swim farther to ice floes where they can hunt their prey. In a December 2005 paper presented at the Society for Marine Mammalogy's sixteenth biennial conference, scientists pointed to the drowning of four polar bears in September 2004 when the sea ice receded an unprecedented 160 miles off the coast of northern Alaska. While this is not yet authoritative proof of the difficulties that receding ice poses, it suggests reason for concern.

Mother polar bears are also having a harder time recovering their lost weight after giving birth, and some scientists believe that the female bear's reproductive life has been shortened and that the task of caring for cubs has become more onerous.

The polar bear may be just the canary in the coal mine. Over the last two decades, scientists have learned substantially more about climate change and the threat that it poses to the world's biodiversity. A consensus has emerged among the scientific community that climate change is the most serious environmental issue that we humans face today. It poses threats to agriculture, particularly in the Southern Hemisphere; to low-lying coasts of almost all countries bordered by oceans; and to biodiversity. It has even been described as a "threat multiplier," in terms of national security, in a 2007 report by the CNA Corporation. In attempting to save the polar bear from extinction, we are investing in our own future as well.

In December 1997, in recognition of these growing environmental threats, more than 160 countries met in Kyoto, Japan, and negotiated a global agreement on climate change. Developed countries agreed to reduce their carbon emissions below their 1990 levels. While the level of reductions varied from country to country (averaging about 8 percent for European countries and 7 percent for the United States), developing countries were not required to reduce carbon emissions to specific targets but did agree to implement policies that would mitigate climate change. The Kyoto Protocol became effective when Russia ratified it in November 2004. As of December 2006, 169 countries have ratified it. Only two developed countries have refused: the United States and Australia.

The United States had been the world's largest emitter of greenhouse gases, but scientists now estimate that it was surpassed by China in 2007. Pulling out of the Kyoto Protocol deeply angered many of our traditional allies, and without the leadership of the

LEFT *A mother polar bear and her new cub; unlike males and nonpregnant females, mother polar bears fast during the winter in their den, losing up to two-thirds of their body weight giving birth and nursing (spring, coastal plain, Arctic National Wildlife Refuge).*

RIGHT *Aerial view of spring ice breakup along the Arctic coast (east of Point Barrow, National Petroleum Reserve–Alaska)*

ABOVE *A sow and cub slide on the ice (autumn, coastal plain, Arctic National Wildlife Refuge).*
Polar bears have an insulating layer of fat up to 4.3 inches thick.

United States, an important opportunity was lost to put in place a global program to address climate change.

In the Intergovernmental Panel on Climate Change's most recent report, released in February 2007, the IPCC scientists concluded with 90 percent certainty that the earth is warming and that human activities contribute in a significant way to that warming. Established in 1988, the IPCC is a joint venture between two United Nations groups: the World Meteorological Organization and the United Nations Environment Programme. The IPCC releases its findings on climate change every five to six years. Many distinguished scientists participate in its deliberations, as do government officials from countries with high fossil-fuel emissions or those dependent on the exports of fossil fuels (such as Saudi Arabia), which for economic reasons are resistant to the introduction of climate change abatement policies. Since the IPCC operates on a consensus basis, its reports are "conservative" and, if anything, may understate the strength of the scientific conclusions. Consequently, its findings are sobering, and they should be taken very seriously.

More troubling even than the IPCC findings are scientific data from a 2004 report by the Arctic Climate Impact Assessment Group, which was not included in the 2007 IPCC study. These data indicate that the rate of climate change is accelerating and that the Arctic is experiencing the most rapid rate of acceleration, thus giving us a smaller window of opportunity in which to address it. Scientists, including those who compiled the latest IPCC assessment, generally agree that we have about two to three decades in which to deal with climate change; after that time, we will have reached a tipping point beyond which meaningful solutions will no longer be possible.

As we progress further into a no-win scenario, feedback loops accelerate the overall rate of climate change. In Greenland, for instance, where the glaciers are more than a mile thick, scientists initially thought that the ice would melt from the top down. This indeed is what occurs. However, scientists did not anticipate that surface water also forms *moulins*, or large holes, in the glaciers; these moulins funnel meltwater down through the glaciers, lubricating the bottom of the ice so that the glaciers flow into the ocean at double their normal speed. In addition, the glaciers have become so fragmented that

SURFACE MELT-INDUCED ACCELERATION OF ICE-SHEET FLOW

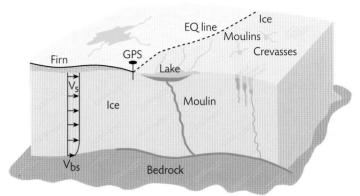

V_s = velocity of ice at surface
V_{bs} = velocity of ice at base (basal sliding)
GPS = a Global Positioning System location
EQ line = equilibrium line; boundary between accumulation area and ablation

SOURCE: "SURFACE MELT-INDUCED ACCELERATION OF GREENLAND ICE-SHEET FLOW,"
BY H. JAY ZWALLY, ET AL., NASA GODDARD SPACE FLIGHT CENTER; U.S. GEOLOGICAL SURVEY

Figure 2. The accumulation area of a glacier is the upper region where snow accumulation exceeds melting; in the ablation area, snow, ice, or water in any form are lost from a glacier. Characteristics of the equilibrium and ablation zones include surface lakes, inflow channels, and moulins *(vertical meltwater tunnels). Basal ice flow is partly from basal sliding and partly from shear deformations.*

Greenland now has "glacier quakes" that register seismically.

On the other side of the world, in Antarctica, the sea ice around that continent, which has acted like a big belt holding the glaciers in place, has melted far faster than anticipated. As a result, glaciers are calving at a much higher rate than anything seen for the past several centuries. The melting of the sea ice surrounding much of Antarctica has also precipitated a rapid decline in ice algae, which in turn support krill. Krill is an essential element in the food chain for much sea life, particularly that in the southern oceans, including penguins, sea lions, and whales. This decline in krill is resulting in a sharp decrease in the Adélie penguin population.

Not only is wildlife affected by the melting sea ice, but the

Five nations have jurisdiction over polar bears: Russia, Norway, Denmark (Greenland), Canada, and the United States. In addition, many bears live on ice floating in international waters.

ABOVE *Grizzlies have long had habitat in the Arctic, mixing territory with polar bears.*

RIGHT *Walruses leave their calves on the pack ice while diving for food in shallow water over the continental shelf; if the ice edge withdraws miles beyond the shelf, young walrus could be abandoned in water thousands of feet deep (springtime, Bering Sea).*

ABOVE *A polar bear sow drags herself across thin, newly formed pack ice, keeping her back legs spread, because if she picked them up, she would fall through the ice (autumn, coastal plain, Arctic National Wildlife Refuge).*

continued melting of Greenland's glaciers, specifically, could raise the level of the planet's oceans by more than 20 feet. Were this to occur, the impact on coastal cities such as New Orleans, London, and Shanghai would be catastrophic. New York's subway system would be flooded. Low-elevation coastal states, such as Florida or Louisiana, would lose significant land mass to a rising ocean. Much of Cape Cod, Martha's Vineyard, and Nantucket would be under water. Rising temperatures due to climate change could also result in increased fires in our western forests and less rainfall in the American Southeast, adversely affecting agriculture in that region. The United States could see a rise in diseases previously found only in the tropics. Dengue fever or malaria could spread from Central or South America to the southern United States. Further, the damage to our biodiversity could be severe. Cold-water fish, such as trout, would see their range substantially reduced, and the icon of New England, the sugar maple, might no longer be found south of the Canadian border. Finally, continued global climate change could precipitate mass emigration from countries such as Bangladesh or parts of China, India, and areas of Africa that might become too arid for farming or livestock grazing. Nations would likely fight over dwindling supplies of freshwater.

The good news is that a political sea change is taking place in this country. States such as California have passed legislation requiring utilities to generate at least 20 percent of their electricity from renewable energy sources by 2010. California has also passed legislation mandating increased fuel efficiency for automobiles sold in the state, and other legislation instructs the California Air Resources Board to develop market mechanisms and regulations that will reduce greenhouse gases by 25 percent by 2020. Former New York governor George Pataki led a regional initiative in which New York and most of the New England states entered into a compact to limit carbon emissions. Similarly, as of July 2007, 637 U.S. mayors have signed a manifesto supporting the Kyoto Protocol and are introducing energy-saving initiatives in their cities, and the number grows every month.

LEFT *Pressure ridges in the pack ice within a lead (springtime, Chukchi Sea)*

RIGHT *A lead begins to form when a crack opens in the pack ice (spring, Chukchi Sea, Point Barrow).*

Equally encouraging, the chief executive officers of some of America's largest companies—General Electric, DuPont, Caterpillar, Alcoa, ConocoPhillips, Duke Energy, General Motors, John Deere, and others—are asking for national leadership on climate change, pledging to support the reduction of greenhouse gases in America by 60 to 80 percent by 2050. These companies are also implementing business strategies that will create technologies to help us and the rest of the world use energy more efficiently, diversify our sources of energy, and develop alternative non-carbon-intensive energy sources. U.S. companies can become the leaders in these new green technologies and, in doing so, can provide jobs for Americans. On Wall Street, hedge funds, private equity firms, and retail and institutional investors are aggressively looking for "green" investments. The capital markets believe that policies to abate climate change are coming in the near future, and these markets will reward companies and investors that correctly anticipate the impact of these policies.

In Washington DC, members of Congress on both sides of the aisle are considering, for the first time, national legislation to reduce greenhouse-gas emissions. Drafting good, environmentally effective legislation will not be easy, however. Effective legislation will require our nation to make profound changes in its use of energy. Policies to achieve meaningful reductions in carbon emissions need to be economically efficient, fair, and transparent. The costs need to be equitably allocated within industries and between different industrial sectors, as well as between our poor and more affluent citizens. We will have to adopt effective conservation measures; dramatically increase our use of renewable energy sources such as biomass, solar, and wind power; and invest heavily in technologies such as carbon capture and sequestration, which allow coal-burning power plants to capture carbon dioxide and permanently embed it in stable geologic formations. As a major contributor to climate change, the United States should explicitly recognize CO_2 as a pollutant with attendant economic and environmental costs. We need to implement climate abatement policies, such as a cap-and-trading regime or a carbon tax, that increase the relative cost of using carbon-intensive energy compared to renewable and nonpolluting sources of energy. We should recognize that the earth's atmosphere is a commons that belongs to

all of the world's citizens and to future generations. It is economically irresponsible to treat the atmosphere as a free garbage dump. This is not a new idea. The Clean Water Act of 1972 was based on the same premise: that the nation's rivers are part of the public commons and should not be used as dumping grounds for pollutants. It would also be worthwhile to look at the possibility of increasing our use of nuclear energy—nuclear power does not produce greenhouse gases, but a satisfactory solution has not yet been found for nuclear waste.

Average Americans are concerned about climate change and are asking what they can do about it. Sales of hybrid gasoline-electric cars are increasing. Households are replacing incandescent bulbs with fluorescent bulbs, installing more insulation to save energy, and using double- and triple-glazed windows. Perhaps most important, people are beginning to educate themselves on steps they can take as individuals to reduce the possibility of long-term climate change.

To successfully address climate change, the United States will have to initiate an economic transformation that will be broader and deeper than the last twenty-five years of economic changes precipitated by globalization. We will no doubt encounter resistance, but I believe that, with the right leadership, the inherent decency of the American people will prevail. We undertook the sacrifices necessary to win World War II, emerging as a far stronger nation. In the past, great leaders have recognized our obligation to future generations and have successfully rallied citizens to act as responsible stewards. If we can save the polar bears, we will ultimately save ourselves.

Theodore Roosevelt IV, a great-grandson of President Theodore Roosevelt, is a managing director at Lehman Brothers, New York. He is also chairman of Lehman Brothers' Council on Climate Change. Roosevelt was a Foreign Service Officer for the Department of State, serving in Washington DC and Ouagadougou, Upper Volta, West Africa (now Burkina Faso). Roosevelt is an active conservationist who is chair of the Pew Center for Global Climate Change, a board member of the Alliance for Climate Protection, a member of the Governing Council of the Wilderness Society, and a trustee for the American Museum of Natural History, the World Resources Institute, and Trout Unlimited. He and his wife, Constance, live in Brooklyn Heights.

ABOVE *Polar bears tend to be more social than grizzly bears, often congregating in groups of unrelated individuals (autumn, coastal plain, Arctic National Wildlife Refuge).*

Steven Kazlowski

PHOTOGRAPHER'S JOURNAL: PHOTOGRAPHER'S JOURNAL: PORTRAIT OF A POLAR BEAR DEN

Thursday, March 23, 2006.
Minus 10 to minus 20 degrees F.
Light 10 mph west wind.

It happened today.

The polar bear mother and cubs came out of their den right in front of us. The light was perfect.

The bears had first emerged from the den four days earlier—but we hadn't gotten a clear view even once, let alone lighting that might make for a good image. Since that day I had lived in fear that they would take off for the sea before we could get a good look at them. But today all the waiting and preparation paid off.

We were camped 60 miles east of Prudhoe Bay and 60 miles west of Kaktovik. The three of us—Jack Kayotuk, Bruce Inglangasak, and I—had arrived seventeen days earlier. Jack and Bruce had agreed to wait with me at the den until the sow emerged with her cubs, which I knew could take up to a month. Jack had returned to town for supplies—and had almost died in the process. His snowmobile had broken down 30 miles from town just before blizzard conditions set in, and he walked the rest of the way, spending one night sleeping in a snowbank. He'd been frostbitten and had stayed in town to recover, a reminder of the inherent danger of living in this landscape of ice and snow.

The key to photographing a mother polar bear and her cubs emerging from their den in the spring is long-term planning—and a lot of luck. It's best to look for a den in the fall, because snow will drift over the entrance during the winter, making it almost impossible to spot a den in spring without disturbing its inhabitants. Then you return to the site in early spring and set up camp far enough away from the den not to disturb the bears, with a snow blind for cover a little closer from which to observe and take photos—and hope for the best.

As you wait, you realize that anything could have happened during the long winter. The den could have collapsed, the sow might have been scared off, or a big male might have dug her out to eat her—an increasing concern with the impacts of climate change on polar bears' normal hunting patterns. Jack and I had spotted this den the previous autumn, in the first week of November, just after the pregnant sow had gone inside. When we returned at the beginning of March, we knew there was no safe way to check whether the bear was still there; we just had to wait.

From the time she had gone into the den, almost five months of Arctic winter had passed. The long days of darkness were becoming shorter and now giving way to light, melding the end of winter with the beginning of springtime. As we went through the slow work of setting up and maintaining our camp—cutting and stacking blocks of hard snow to make an *iglu* for use as a blind, melting snow for water, keeping a watchful eye on fuel use while trying to stay warm—I was grateful for the faint scent of spring in the air, but I was aware that all our efforts and the long wait could be for nothing.

When we awoke this morning, we saw that the harsh winds had blown the snow away in patches, exposing frozen dirt and gravel that would be picked up by the high winds and sandblasted across the coast. The day was gorgeous, a clean sunrise, with a lot of moisture in the air in the form of ice fog. It hit the ground as fresh frost, covering what had been dirty snow with a brilliant white blanket.

By 7:00 AM we were at the blind. Bruce started the stove in the *iglu*—and the next thing I knew, there was moisture in my lens. This was bad. We shut the stove down and I put the lens outside to cool.

LEFT *This unusual image shows a partially dug polar bear den. The pregnant sow abandoned this attempt, probably because the snow was too shallow, and went elsewhere to dig her den.*

LEFT *Bruce Inglangasak and Jack Kayotuk put the finishing touches on the iglu that will be used as a photography blind.*

RIGHT *Bruce Inglangasak builds a snow wall around the tent to buffer the campsite from 60- to 70-mile-an-hour winds at minus 40° F.*

The previous morning, my preferred lens for this kind of work—a 500 millimeter—had heated too fast and had cracked. It wasn't entirely unusable, but now it had a problem with focus.

The strikes against us were mounting, and the obstacles of this improbable trip were finally beginning to affect me. The uncertain waiting, the severe cold, the lack of funds, the very real likelihood that the bears were long gone, and now lens difficulties...What had made me think I could do this? I felt very low at this point, which added to my anxiety about whether I would get any photos on this trip at all.

The only choice I had was to keep going. I attached my 80–200 millimeter lens with a 1.4 teleconverter to the camera and raised it to the window in the wall of the *iglu*.

In a matter of minutes, the sow lumbered out of the top hole of the den.

I quickly took some shots, but I was too far away to get effective images with the lens I was using. I asked Bruce to grab my 500 millimeter lens, which we had put outside to defog. Luckily, the fog was off the inside element, so I was able to use it. I could only hope the focus problem wouldn't have too much effect.

Then the two cubs came out. They started sliding down the hill, and the mother rolled on her back with the cubs tumbling around her. The cubs nursed and played, and mom kept an eye on us. Then she headed back to the den for a nap, the cubs following her inside.

At 1:30 PM she came back out of the side hole. It was minus 15 degrees Fahrenheit in the *iglu*, and I had been keeping the camera's battery warm in my glove. I took it out of my glove and slammed it into the camera, photographing the mother bear and her cubs for a while. They stayed close to the den, roaming in and out of our sight all day.

RIGHT *Guide and friend Jack Kayotuk*

ABOVE *A newly built polar bear den in the fall; the pregnant female has just entered her den. Her cubs will be born, typically in a litter of two, in midwinter, weighing less than 2 pounds, blind, and completely helpless; they will nurse and grow in the safety of the sealed den.*

CLOCKWISE FROM TOP LEFT
Emerging from the den for a first look at the world; new spring cubs weigh around 15 or 20 pounds when they first come out of the den, a year after conception. / Out in the bright light after wintering in the den / The mother bears stretches and cleans herself by rolling on the snow after being in the den all winter. / Female polar bears, which reach an average age of thirty, have their first cubs at around age six, followed by new litters about every three years.

The bears were amazing—the mother polar bear is all that is wild. She sniffed the wind, squinting her eyes, trying to get used to the light. The cubs were pure white with big black eyes, and they seemed to have endless energy. They were two bundles of love and hell at once. They bounded up to Mom and pawed her in the face, and then she gave way to nursing—around and around they went. To see this was to witness strength, love, joy, humor, danger, intelligence, and ferocity all in the same moment.

She knew she was being watched. The entire time I was shooting, I could tell by her look that we were not to leave the *iglu* and come nearer to her. She seemed to accept our presence as long as we stuck to the program.

It was a long, cold day, and by 6:00 PM the light was gone. We could see both the top and side entrances of the den, and we knew the bears hadn't gone back inside. Bruce said that polar bears fresh out of their den head toward the sea when they get that first whiff of salt water, and we wondered if they were already gone. We headed back to camp for the night, warmed up, downloaded chips and looked at the pictures, and got ready for the next day.

Friday, March 24, 2006
Minus 25 degrees F
10 mph wind from the west

The sun was behind the clouds when we headed over to the blind at 7:30 AM. At 10:00 AM the sow appeared, using the side door, not the top.

There was still frost and moisture in the air, so we kept the camera gear cold and tried to block our breath so it wouldn't frost up the lenses. Mother bear wandered to the top of the hill in plain sight, with the light just breaking through the clouds. One cub joined her, and the sow began eating small, exposed tufts of grass in order to

The total world population of polar bears is estimated at 21,000 to 25,000 animals. That estimate includes solid numbers from Canada and the United States and very uncertain figures from Russia, where research is sparse and enforcement of hunting prohibitions is weak.

CLOCKWISE FROM TOP LEFT
Nestled together / Nursing is a frequent activity; during her cubs' first year, a mother polar bear's hunting time is curtailed while she raises her cubs. / Exploring new surroundings / Staying close. A female polar bear has cubs only about five times in her life—a very slow reproductive rate imposed by the stringent demands of the Arctic environment.

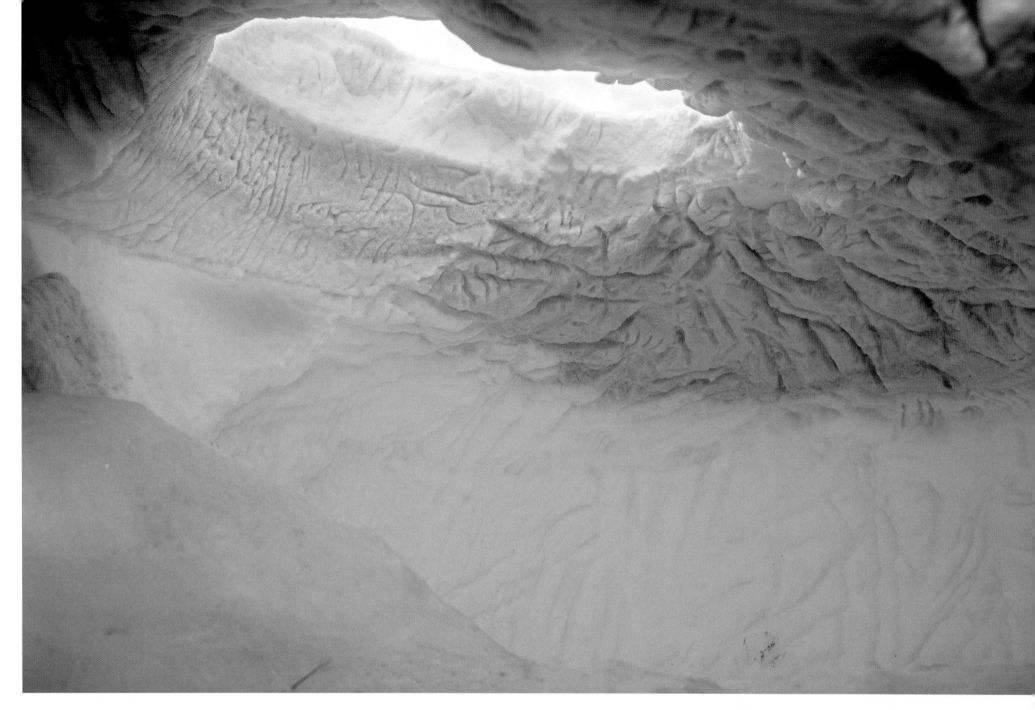

ABOVE *A rare opportunity to look inside a polar bear den. Note the claw marks around the opening.*

CLOCKWISE FROM TOP LEFT
The sow eats grass to help stimulate her digestive system. / The new family outside their den / After watching, one of the cubs begins eating grass, too. / Among polar bears, only pregnant females hibernate, going into a slowed physiological state after giving birth.

help stimulate her digestive system. Then the other cub joined them. Sometime later we watched as they ambled together, as a family, toward the east side of the draw, out of view.

We were silent as we waited, moving our feet to stay warm, listening to the ever-present wind. Eventually a red fox wandered into sight. It sniffed around the den, marked the spot, and explored the area slowly, not running away as it would have if the bears were still there—and then we realized the tale had been told.

We went over to the den and then followed three sets of bear tracks that crossed over the top of the bank, descended to within 80 feet of our camp, and then disappeared into the white blend of sky and snow as they headed straight out to sea. The bears were gone.

With exhausted relief, we went back to the den—and crawled inside.

Not all polar bears hibernate—only pregnant females, which go into dens to give birth and then go into a slowed physiological state. The little ones are perhaps more active during the denning period, feeding off their mother's milk, growing, and playing. It was obvious from the many different chambers the sow had made that she had spent a great deal of time awake inside the den with the cubs. It did not smell, and there were no feces in evidence. Neither, interestingly, was there hair. It was a tight fit, making it difficult to get around inside the den. It had partially collapsed in places, and claw marks everywhere showed how she had carved it out. It looked like several connected dens, as if when one area started to collapse or she wanted to move, she would make a tunnel and dig out a new den.

The sow had stayed at the den site for six days from when she broke ground, statistically within the average range of time that scientists have observed, before heading to the sea. The experience was more than I could have hoped for, and we accomplished it without disturbing either the mother polar bear or her cubs. What an exhilarating feeling! We left the den and walked back to camp, ready to head back to the village.

A great wildlife picture happens when multiple forms of energy come together at one point in time for a fraction of a second. The trick is to meet this moment and capture it. Like the bears themselves, the photographs on these pages, to me, are something close to miraculous. I got these images by a slim margin—against the odds, in spite of a broken lens, bad weather, and the near loss of one of our friends. God gave us a gift but kept us honest.

LEFT *Heading out to sea; after first emerging from the den, a sow and cubs will leave the site in two days to three weeks, in correlation with ringed seal pupping.*

While climate scientists disagree whether an ice-free Arctic might come in forty years or a hundred, polar bears might be gone sooner.

Charles Wohlforth

On Thin Ice: Polar Bears in the Changing Arctic

OFF POINT BARROW, AT ALASKA'S NORTHERN tip, where the Beaufort and Chukchi seas meet, our open boat of Iñupiaq hunters lurched atop the opaque gray mass of a wave as high as a man, crashed down on the far side, collided with another wave from a different direction, and lurched up again. The pack ice had withdrawn hundreds of miles from shore that September, farther than ever before measured. Wind across the expanse of unfrozen water built steep, chaotic waves at the meeting place of the two seas, waves too large for even our sturdy fiberglass craft. The outboard motor pushed us forward a jolt at a time toward the safety of Elson Lagoon, behind the point, as the afternoon darkened and the sky's ragged overcast strewed random snowflakes into the wind.

Rounding the point, I peered over the backs of waves breaking onto the dark pea gravel of the beach. Point Barrow, the continent's final gesture to the Arctic Ocean, is nothing more than a shoal breaching the surface of the water, a miles-long pile of rock that has been crushed fine by the weather. Hardly anyone goes there, but the previous fall Iñupiaq whalers had used this desolate spot to leave a bone pile of hunting spoils. A year later, the easy food may have attracted polar bears that normally keep to the floating pack ice. When the ice suddenly retreated northward, the bears were stranded. On islands to the east, I'd counted thirty-five bears standing forlornly along miles of a foggy, windswept gravel barrier island, spaced as far apart as their solitary nature demanded. As we rounded the point in the waves, I saw more polar bears grouped near the waste pile, coats stained by the dirty ground or the bloody bones. One rushed fiercely toward the white foam of the incoming breakers as if to challenge the sea.

The sea is a polar bear's home. Polar bears (*Ursus maritimus*) are classified as marine mammals and can spend their entire lives of around twenty-five to thirty years on the water. But the water is usually frozen. They swim well, but mostly amid floating ice where the open leads tend to be calm—not for long distances in rough seas. Polar bears hunt by stealth, catching seals hauled out on the ice or coming to breathing holes for air. They have little chance of catching a speedy, deep-diving seal in open water. On solid ice, however, polar bears are terrifying: exquisitely adapted to creeping among jumbled, angular white blocks while silent and nearly invisible, even to human beings. To pick up the sight of an approaching bear, you must stand still and wait for the animal's movement as a clue to the visual puzzle it presents.

The strange congregation of dozens of stranded bears that I saw near the town of Barrow in the fall of 2002 threw the community into fear and consternation. A 1,100-pound bear—a large male—was shot when it wouldn't leave the school. Visitors were warned not to walk outdoors. Biologists employed by the local government were constantly on the run to keep polar bears off the streets. Polar bears normally don't eat people, but they easily can and, when hungry enough, they occasionally have. Bears on land in the summer and fall have been more common all along the coast since the trend of warmer weather shortened the winters and diminished the sea ice. But no one had ever seen an invasion like this before. Biologists counted more than one hundred bears near town. Yet most scientists declined to blame climate change. While the unprecedented withdrawal of the ice was indisputable, how the ice movement affected the bears remained a subject of debate. After all, there seemed to be plenty of bears around.

Elsewhere in the polar bear's range, however, the picture was already clearer, thanks to the pioneering work of a hearty biologist,

LEFT *Adult polar bear; a polar bear's sense of smell is so acute, it can sniff out a carcass or a seal breathing hole up to a mile away.*

LEFT *King eiders during spring migration (near Point Barrow)*

RIGHT *The ice recedes offshore of Barrow, Alaska, population about 4,500, in early summer.*

ABOVE *Polar bears prey on bearded seals, which weigh an average of 750 pounds (coastal area, Arctic National Wildlife Refuge, Brooks Range in the distance).*

Ian Stirling, of the Canadian Wildlife Service. Stirling is the proto-typical rugged outdoor wildlife scientist, practical and direct. After thirty-seven years and nearing retirement, he still spends two or three months a year in the field, often working from remote tent camps or shacks in minus-30-degree Fahrenheit temperatures—and in his leisure time, nearer Edmonton, Alberta, goes camping, fishing, and cross-country skiing. Stirling began wondering in the 1970s how ice conditions that vary over decades could affect marine mammal numbers. He had been to Antarctica, where seal populations seemed to rise and fall with changes in the ice. If similar variations were hap-pening to Canadian polar bears, hunting quotas based on a string of good ice years might be too high for the bad years.

Establishing a link between the quality of sea ice habitat and polar bear numbers would be difficult and would take a long time. Polar bears live long and reproduce slowly—at best, a female can rear cubs only every three years—but they are adapted to ride out a few bad years of poorer health without losing many animals. Bears mate on the sea ice in the spring, and pregnant females enter dens in the fall to have their young. When the cubs are born in midwinter, typically in a litter of two, they're under 2 pounds, blind, and completely help-less. In the safety of the sealed den, they nurse and grow, reaching 15 or 25 pounds by the time they and the mother emerge in the spring, a year after conception. Because her fetuses and cubs are so small, a pregnant female doesn't invest much in their growth before they are born—it's nursing them that uses up all her energy—so if times are tough, a polar bear can abort or reabsorb her fetus, or fail to produce milk for a nursing cub, saving fat reserves to assure her own survival and to breed another year. If resources do permit a success-ful birth, a young polar bear stays with its mother for twenty-eight months, or two entire winter seasons, after leaving the den. As with any long-lived animal with slow reproduction, polar bears cannot withstand much hunting, and their numbers were depleted before an international agreement protected them in the 1970s. After hunting pressure let up, they began to come back.

LEFT *A sow stands to see what's coming her way (autumn, coastal plain, Arctic National Wildlife Refuge.*

Biologists in Alaska have captured polar bears they estimated at more than 1,750 pounds.

ABOVE *Surveying the spring landscape from a giant iceberg in the Chukchi Sea*

RIGHT *Ian Stirling, a pioneering polar bear biologist with the Canadian Wildlife Service for more than three decades, tags polar bear blood samples (Herschel Island, Yukon Territory).*

A study relating ice extent and bear numbers would require annual counts and physical measurements over many years to track the bears' health and reproductive success. Such work is expensive and physically demanding, and Stirling couldn't get funding to do it over the long term. Government agencies usually prefer granting money to answer particular questions in three years or less, not open-ended spending. Stirling's solution, fitting a frugal and energetic personality, was to organize many different projects in the same place, each contributing separately to a data set that would eventually span many years and answer the larger question. He chose to study western Hudson Bay, near the southern end of the polar bear range. Besides answering wildlife management questions near Churchill, Manitoba, the studies there would be easier than elsewhere because an entire population of bears tends to spend summer onshore—and white bears stand out on green tundra better than on white snow.

Andrew Derocher became one of the graduate students Stirling brought on in the 1980s to keep his many related projects staffed and funded. With a thick brown beard and a face darkly tanned by sun on snow, Derocher looks as much the outdoor type as his mentor. Together, they tried to understand why the polar bears of western Hudson Bay were getting skinnier in every category of sex and age. Derocher recalled, "All the bears in the population were declining, without exception. And no matter how we looked at that data, that wasn't disappearing. They were all declining."

The team looked at pollution, hunting, and other possible causes, setting aside climate because they believed the climate would vary from year to year and wouldn't explain the one-way trend they were seeing. Stirling said, "It seemed to me that something was happening. But initially I wasn't sure if that was part of the long-term picture or annual variation...I'm a fairly conservative scientist, and I like to think about things for a long time." Only in 1993—after more than a decade of study—did Stirling and Derocher feel comfortable enough to publish a paper relating bear weight and reproductive success to the time of the annual ice breakup on Hudson Bay. In 1999, Stirling and

LEFT *Sunset, autumn, full moon rising (coastal plain, Arctic National Wildlife Refuge)*

RIGHT *Curious cub plays tag with the photographer (autumn, coastal plain, Arctic National Wildlife Refuge)*

RIGHT *A Canadian icebreaker (summer, Chukchi Sea, near the National Petroleum Reserve–Alaska)*

LEFT *Young walruses are sometimes attacked by polar bears, but the adults' formidable tusks are often fatal to a hungry bear.*

ABOVE *A big bowhead whale flips its tail fluke as it dives (Chukchi Sea, near Point Barrow).*

another pair of colleagues made the case airtight, publishing a paper in the journal *Arctic* that showed a nineteen-year record of declining indices of bear condition that matched with ice reductions. Although they found no loss in the number of bears, they predicted one.

But that research had surprisingly little immediate impact. Scientists felt the situation in Manitoba simply wasn't similar to what was happening off the northern Arctic coast, where most polar bears live. The spring breakup of sea ice in western Hudson Bay tends to strand bears onshore, where they fast until the bay refreezes in the fall and restores access to their prey—seals. In the Beaufort and Chukchi seas, ice also withdraws from the shoreline in spring, but it persists offshore through the summer, a vast floating continent where bears continue hunting year-round. The polar bear population seemed strong, and it was possible that thinning ice could, in some places, even make the ecosystem richer and the hunting easier.

Climate change impact on polar bears would be difficult to detect in the Alaskan Arctic, in part because no one had made continuous, long-term measurements specifically designed to look at the issue, as Ian Stirling has done in Canada. Besides, at the rate of change then projected by atmospheric scientists, effects like those in western Hudson Bay could be many years away. In 2001, Steve Amstrup, a top polar bear biologist for the U.S. Geological Survey (USGS), told me the problem remained in the realm of speculation in Alaska.

"How do you study it?" Amstrup said. "We're talking about changes that occur over decades. The only way to study it is to make sure you have long-term, ongoing studies, and unfortunately, government budgets don't work that way. You get money one year at a time."

Amstrup was already thinking, however, about how to use old data to look at this issue. The polar bear's status had become a frequent question because of other changes in the Arctic ecosystem that were already evident to indigenous people and some far-sighted scientists. Again, long-term data held the key. Jackie Grebmeier, a University of Tennessee oceanographer, had developed a fifteen-year record of northern Bering Sea ecology in a way similar to Stirling's approach with bears: she won grants for many different projects, year after year, that would take her on icebreakers returning to the same waters off northern Alaska annually. Over time she saw the seafloor

ecosystem diminishing: less biomass, smaller organisms, and a 90 percent decline in bottom-feeding eider ducks in the area she studied.

Grebmeier linked these changes to the withdrawal of the sea ice. The ice edge is a rich habitat, green with algae underneath and harboring its own ecological community of tiny animals and the uniquely adapted Arctic cod, which lives nowhere else. Biological activity peaks in spring and summer, as the ice melts. Organic matter at the ice edge falls to the seafloor of the continental shelf, a few hundred feet deep, powering a food web for diving animals, including gray whales, walruses, and bearded seals. But as the ice edge has withdrawn from the continental shelf, it has dropped less of its store of food energy into those shallow waters. Beyond the shelf, the seafloor falls off steeply to thousands of feet deep. Potential food that falls there sinks into an abyss, too dark for much life and too deep for diving animals.

By the end of the 1990s, Grebmeier had enough evidence to win National Science Foundation funding for a ten-year program of dedicated icebreaker cruises and analysis called the Shelf-Basin Interactions Project. But by the time the project's first icebreaker set sail in the spring of 2002, it hardly needed to break any ice. At the time of year when the ice edge should have been doing its biological magic, it had largely withdrawn from the shelf, leaving the ship often steaming through open water. That year and each that followed, the sea ice withdrew to unprecedented distances from Alaska. The shrinkage of the entire northern ice pack repeatedly set new records.

During their 2004 voyage, as Grebmeier's team sailed in water as deep as 10,000 feet, they encountered juvenile walruses nine times, widely spread out and alone without their mothers. Normally, walruses rear their young for two years, keeping them on ice while diving for food or carrying them on their backs for surface swims. But the nearest adults the crew saw were many miles toward shore, over the continental shelf in 300 feet of water or less. Research doesn't exist to document the broad effects of reduced ice on walruses, but Grebmeier's cruise showed what could happen. Apparently, the ice had pulled too far from the animals' seafloor food source, forcing them to abandon their young. The baby walruses, alone over the oceanic abyss, were doomed.

"They wanted to get on the boat," Grebmeier said. "We'd have to

NORTHERN HEMISPHERE SEA ICE EXTENT, SEPTEMBER 2007

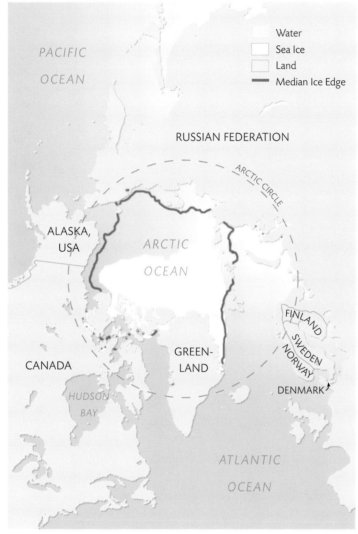

Water
Sea Ice
Land
— Median Ice Edge

PACIFIC
OCEAN

RUSSIAN FEDERATION

ARCTIC CIRCLE

ALASKA,
USA

ARCTIC
OCEAN

FINLAND

SWEDEN
NORWAY

GREEN-
LAND

CANADA

DENMARK

HUDSON
BAY

ATLANTIC
OCEAN

SOURCE: F. FETTERER, K. KNOWLES, AND STAFF, NATIONAL SNOW AND ICE
DATA CENTER, NOAA

*Figure 3. In September 2007, the Arctic sea-ice edge had retreated signifi-
cantly from the median September monthly extent , which is based on data
from 1979 to 2000. The total extent of the Arctic sea ice was 1.59 million
square miles in 2007; the previous record low was 2.05 million square miles
in 2005. The long-term average minimum is 2.60 million square miles.*

launch small boats at times, and the little walruses would follow. It was
a heart-wrenching type of thing, but there's nothing you can do about
that. It's not like you can pick up these stranded animals out at sea."

Polar bears' most important prey is the ringed seal, which eats
Arctic cod, followed by the bottom-foraging bearded seal. No one
has ever counted these ice seals with any precision, so there's no
direct way of knowing if their numbers have risen or fallen. Native
hunters and their scientific colleagues with the Alaska Department
of Fish and Game report that the seals they catch near shore seem
healthy enough. But a reduced seafloor food supply seems likely to
affect bearded seals, and the loss of ice that harbors Arctic cod would
affect the ringed seals. Besides their food supply being affected,
ringed seals might have trouble reproducing. They give birth in dens
of snow built over breathing holes on the shorefast ice, warm shelters
where they feed and protect vulnerable pups for six weeks. Disinte-
grating spring ice could expose the young. Thinner snow could make
for weaker caves. Ian Stirling observed that unseasonable rain collapsed ringed seal dens, and the pups were scooped up by predators.

But even if seals remain plentiful, how will polar bears catch them
when the ice pulls far from shore for ever longer periods? The rapid
shrinkage of summer sea ice has astonished scientists, who never predicted such a quick response to global warming. Native elders never
saw anything like it happening before, nor does their oral tradition
relate such changes.

The strange behavior of the polar bears adds another unfamiliar
element. On the Chukchi and Beaufort sea coasts, they were seldom seen onshore in the summer as late as the 1980s. Now they
commonly show up in summer on the narrow barrier islands that
outline the coast, mere wisps of land that offer little more than solid
ground on which to stand. Scott Schliebe, of the U.S. Fish and Wildlife
Service, supervised a study beginning in 2000 to find out if ice conditions explained why residents of Alaska's northern coast were seeing
so many more polar bears onshore. The team's sightings of stranded
bears matched with how far the ice edge stood from shore: the farther the ice receded, the more bears there were on land. Still, no one
knows why this is so. Has the ice withdrawn beyond the bears' food
supply? Do they somehow know it is too far to swim? Are females

Radio-tracked bears in the Chukchi Sea traveled more than 3,400 miles a year. In spring, the Chukchi bears moved north 9 miles a day, while the ice they walked on was moving 9 miles a day in the opposite direction.

ABOVE *Sea ice may freeze flat, but it is soon broken, stacked, and twisted by the immense forces of currents, wind, and atmospheric pressure; the brine is sometimes squeezed out, and the Iñupiat melt the resulting freshwater ice for drinking water.*

RIGHT *A polar bear with an ear tagged rests on frozen tundra (autumn, coastal plain, Arctic National Wildlife Refuge).*

landing early to enter dens and birth their young, knowing they otherwise could be stranded far out at sea?

Polar bears can swim a long way. They're buoyant and well insulated. In calm water, a healthy adult may be able to paddle for 100 miles. But there must be a limit. Craig George, one of those Barrow biologists responsible for keeping bears out of town, has seen exhausted bears show up on the beach after swims that must have been 100 miles or more.

He offered this description of one incident: "I vividly remember a female with her two cubs that swam ashore near town. We repelled her several times with cracker shells back into the ocean, but where was she realistically to go, with the sea ice over 200 miles away? Dodging cracker shells, she came ashore a third time and walked right through our crowd of dissuaders, crossed the beach road, and lay down with her cubs, barely 100 yards from the beach and only 10 yards from the road. She seemed to say, 'Shoot me if you must, but I ain't moving. If I go back to sea, I'm dead anyway...' So there she lay with her cubs for two days, barely moving a muscle. Hundreds of vehicles surrounded her day and night; the little family was quite the spectacle. But no one shot her, and finally, after two days of comatose rest, she slowly got up and ambled up the coast with her cubs to spend the rest of the fall on the tundra. We never saw her again."

Polar bears' big, flat front paws work like paddles to push water when they swim. At the zoo in Anchorage, Alaska, you can see a polar bear through glass as it dives underwater—the big paws make the water into a ladder as the bear rises and descends. But while camped on the shore ice with Iñupiaq hunters, when I saw bears swimming it was the animals' ease and grace that impressed me. After midnight the sun was low and golden; the ice where we stood and the floe on the far side of the open lead were pale blue; the strip of water itself, rippling here and there with an unfelt breeze, graded in color from black to a romantic royal blue. A polar bear cruised into view, swimming along the lead like a canal boat, carrying a cub on her back, gliding steadily north. An hour behind her, another bear arrived in front of us. It stopped and held place in the water, craning its neck like a periscope to scan the ice and our camp. The bear moved as if its body swam separately within its loose coat: the bear's neck,

stretching impossibly long and high for the view, left the animal's great mass far behind in the water.

In September 2004 the water was glassy calm for hundreds of miles over the Beaufort Sea north of the eastern edge of Alaska. "It was the kind of weather where you could be out there in a canoe," recalled marine ecologist Charles Monnett. He lay on his stomach peering out the bubble window of a twin-engine aircraft looking for bowhead whales—part of an annual aerial count conducted by the U.S. Minerals Management Service. Ice was nowhere in sight, but a white spot came into view. It was a polar bear, swimming miles offshore, toward the sea, with no ice ahead of it for scores of miles. The biologists noted the bear in their records, then saw another and another. "The funny thing about this kind of research is that you don't always know it when you see something significant," Monnett said, but after seeing about ten bears miles offshore—including a sow with cubs—the biologists realized something unusual was happening. In its previous seventeen years of flights, the whale survey had detected only a dozen bears swimming offshore.

Bad weather grounded the survey project. Strong winds whipped up waves that crashed ashore. Monnett's team didn't get back to the same area of the Beaufort Sea for two weeks. When they did, they again saw a white object floating in the water, but this time it didn't look exactly like a bear—more like a white hump shaped like the arch of a floating tire, or, as Monnett realized, like the backs of the dead otters he had seen as a researcher during the 1989 *Exxon Valdez* oil spill, the animals' heads and paws hanging down into the sea. The team documented the drowned bear and documented three more (a fifth sighting was not confirmed). Monnett remembered the last dead bear, which was bloated, standing out for miles in the low evening sunshine like a beacon. Three of the drowned bears were more than 20 miles from shore, and one was more than 60 miles out; the ice edge lay another 90 to 150 miles beyond their floating remains. There may have been many more dead bears out of sight—the survey pattern made it extremely unlikely the team would have seen them all, and it was unlikely as well that these were the exact same bears they had seen swimming two weeks earlier. No one had ever recorded seeing drowned bears floating in the ocean before, but it made sense: although able to swim far in smooth water, a bear in a storm would struggle for air amid foam, spray, and breaking waves.

Before the warming trend of the last two decades, big waves weren't so common here. Sea ice commonly covered much of the coastal ocean off northern Alaska in the fall, leaving less exposed water to generate waves in the storms that roar through at that time of year. The liquid sea all but disappears when winter sets in, and the shore and ocean become a single plain of white, leaving only narrow leads of smooth, dark water. Even then, the ice is dynamic, constantly responding to the hidden motions of the sea. Polar bears are accustomed to these movements: to stay in their familiar hunting grounds, they constantly hike in the opposite direction of the ice's drift.

If your experience of sea ice comes from the movies, it's easy to imagine it as a Styrofoam-like substance as flat and uniform as a swimming pool deck. But sea ice isn't at all like lake ice. It may freeze as flat as liquid water, but it is soon broken, stacked, and twisted by the immense forces of currents, wind, and atmospheric pressure acting across floes the size of states. Collisions grind up rubble that freezing glues back together into new textures. Rips in the ice open up corridors of water that refreeze into flat new ice, which then may be recompressed into broken shards. The largest seams, where ice crashes together, are called pressure ridges and look like miniature mountain ranges. Ridges may grow large enough to last through the summer's melt, becoming smoothed hills of ice, glowing blue and, thanks to the melting out of brine, fresh—the Iñupiat use multiyear ice to make tea. The ice pack's grinding, mountain building, and erosion resemble a fast-motion version of the earth's geology, with its tectonic plates and continental shelves. Indeed, these ice forms inspired the scientist who first proposed the theory of continental drift. Traveling on the ice feels like traveling on land—it's solid and rough, you often can't see far, and the edge looks like a shoreline. But occasionally you'll encounter a seal breathing hole where all else is white and dry and realize you are over deep water.

Living things need the right kind of ice. Thick rafts of multiyear ice make poor habitat for bears or seals because getting to the water below is too difficult. Thinner ice, near the edge of the pack, harbors the most life, with more light able to get through and with easier passage for animals above and below the water. Bears do best here, near shore, among the greatest concentrations of seals and with ideal conditions for traveling and swimming between floes, bergs, and denning areas onshore. But Monnett fears that this edge ice—which has been weaker and patchier in recent years—may make polar bears particularly vulnerable to storms. In 2005 and 2006, fall blows demolished ice edge areas, apparently dunking bears and stranding them on the beach. "You've got the potential for large areas of ice to shear off or just separate and move away, which can lead to a situation like we saw [in 2006], only more so, where you have a big bunch of ice, with bears on it, a hundred miles away from anything," Monnett said. "Then if you get high winds and rough seas, you have the potential to dump a lot of bears in the water, literally in a day, just overnight... I really think this is a potential mechanism for a real disaster."

No one knows if such a catastrophe has happened before, perhaps during a past warm spell. We do know, however, that polar bears have lived only during times when the earth has been cool enough for polar ice. Genetic studies show they are recent arrivals on the planet, having evolved from brown (or grizzly) bears around 250,000 years ago. A sparse fossil record reaching back just 80,000 years doesn't contradict that finding, and the close relationship is further confirmed by the ability of polar bears and brown bears to mate and produce young that are also capable of reproduction. Studies of past climate, using drilling cores of ancient ice, show that the earth has been cool enough to sustain an Arctic ice pack—and much cooler—for more than half a million years, well before the time of polar bears. The carbon dioxide in the atmosphere, the primary driver of climate warming, now is 35 percent higher than at any time during that period. Polar bears have never faced what's coming.

Polar bears moved to the ocean, and left brown bears behind on land, for access to the prodigious energy supply of seal blubber. An adult polar bear needs an average of 4.4 pounds of seal fat a day to survive. When a bear kills a seal, it usually strips the fat from under its skin, leaving the rest of the carcass for scavengers. The ultimate source of this fat layer—this energy reservoir—is the huge marine

RIGHT *A polar bear sow with a cub in tow swims toward the summer pack ice (Chukchi Sea).*

RIGHT *During the 1980s, polar bears in Canada's western Hudson Bay declined in size and in numbers; a decade later, polar bears in the Alaskan Arctic began to decline as well. This extremely skinny bear had difficulty finding food (springtime).*

LEFT *These are the remains of a young polar bear that probably starved (summer, coastal area, Arctic National Wildlife Refuge). Many young bears three to five years old, recently cut loose by their mother, die of starvation.*

ecosystem from which seals feed by the hundreds of thousands. The shore, by contrast, is a poorer, harsher environment. The relative sizes of the cousin bear species reflect this difference. Male polar bears in Alaska have measured more than 1,700 pounds, and an average adult male weighs roughly 1,000 pounds (females are about half the size of males). The largest brown bears in southern Alaska sometimes grow nearly to polar bear size by eating fatty salmon returning from the sea, but there is no land-based substitute for a food source like the seal. In the Arctic and Alaska's Interior, distant from big salmon runs, male brown bears average around 400 pounds and are sparsely distributed, surviving on vegetation and small mammals such as ground squirrels—their claws are well adapted for digging. Polar bears occasionally occupy brown bear habitat in the Arctic, but they are no competitor for their terrestrial ancestor. Even if the huge polar bear could dig up a ground squirrel with its paddle-like paws or could eat berries with sharp teeth fully adapted to a pure meat diet, it couldn't satisfy the huge energy demands of its blubber-dependent body with small pieces of low-calorie food. In studies on captive bears, they simply couldn't eat the stuff fast enough.

Canadian biologist Derocher has little patience for those who suggest that polar bears can survive the loss of sea ice by adapting to life on land, like their ancestors of a hundred millennia ago. "By that logic," he said, "I should be able to swing tree to tree in a few months if I just put my mind to it."

But the Arctic marine environment, too, may become leaner as the ocean warms. Oceanographer Grebmeier has found that as warmer waters are moving north and ice is retreating in the Bering Sea, west of Alaska, that ecosystem is transforming. Marine mammals that feed on the bottom or at the ice edge are being replaced by fish such as pollock, halibut, and even salmon. As the line of warming climate continues northward into the Chukchi Sea and, perhaps, into the broader Arctic Ocean, walruses, whales, seals, and their predators could be outcompeted by carnivorous fish that previously couldn't survive in those waters. Warmer, ice-free seas might produce more plankton to support the food web than in the past, but the food web they'd support could look more like that of the North Pacific than the Arctic Ocean.

In 2004 Derocher, Stirling, and Nick Lunn, another former Stirling student, published a paper in *Integrative and Comparative Biology* that explained the many threats to the polar bear and its possible trajectory to extinction. The fate of the polar bear also became a key sound bite during the release that fall of a four-year study written by three hundred scientists from all the Arctic nations—the Arctic Climate Impact Assessment—when study chair Bob Corell highlighted the bear issue as a symbol of many changes in his media interviews and marathon public-speaking tours. Still, no evidence had been published that numbers of bears had actually declined.

Attorneys at the Center for Biological Diversity, based in California, read the new findings about polar bears in 2004 and thought they might present grounds to petition for a "threatened" listing under the Endangered Species Act, even if no loss of bears had been documented. When a species is listed under the act, the federal government is required to protect the species when it makes decisions on projects or issues environmental permits. For example, if a proposed dam would damage habitat for a listed fish, a permit to build could not be granted unless the harm could be avoided. In the case of the polar bear, if human-caused global warming were destroying the polar bears' ice habitat, then Endangered Species Act listing might limit federal decisions on projects that would aggravate warming—such as new coal-fired power plants or oil drilling that would increase greenhouse-gas emissions. With a ruling by the U.S. Department of the Interior that the polar bear was threatened—meaning it was on a path to becoming endangered with extinction—then environmental attorneys would have legal grounds to challenge new carbon-emitting projects all over the United States.

Center for Biological Diversity attorney Brendan Cummings originally had the idea years earlier of using the law to force government and the public to address climate change, said his colleague, Kassie Siegel. The problem was finding the right species. First the center considered the Glacier Bay wolf spider: too obscure. Then the Kittlitz's murrelet, which mostly lives near Alaskan glaciers. That case was strong, but the Fish and Wildlife Service put the petition in administrative purgatory, saying it didn't have resources to study the species. Two kinds of coral were a win, but the corals have many threats other than climate change, so the message was muted. When the center and its allies decided to concentrate on the polar bear in 2004, Siegel didn't expect to have the petition approved by the Bush administration's Interior Department. Instead, she thought the administration, which consistently denied the human cause of global warming, would turn down the petition and the center would then have to sue. But that wouldn't be all bad: Siegel looked forward to her day in court to lay out the evidence for climate change, and a win would mean a judge could order the polar bear to be listed as threatened. "It was the best opportunity to litigate what this administration says is the best available science on global warming," Siegel said.

What Siegel hadn't counted on was the extraordinary effort that government field scientists were ready to put into establishing proof of the threat to the polar bear. Scott Schliebe, the U.S. Fish and Wildlife Service biologist in Alaska, was assigned to complete a one-year study of the available science on the polar bear and climate change that the Interior Department would use to decide whether to list the bear as threatened. Schliebe had been studying polar bears since 1980, and although he was as cautious as any government scientist in avoiding talking about his emotions or views, it was obvious the animals and their environment concerned him deeply. Working with intense focus and well beyond the usual government employee's eight-hour day, Schliebe's team gathered all the relevant information from a broad range of specialties and synthesized it into a powerful 262-page document that read like a textbook about climate change effects on polar bears. The document included the Fish and Wildlife Service's own research but also pulled together other findings—from Stirling, Derocher, Monnett, Amstrup, and others—into a single compelling story. "I thought it was our obligation to do the best job we could," Schliebe said.

Meanwhile, more evidence accumulated to support Siegel's petition. USGS biologist Steve Amstrup had been concerned in 2001 about the lack of long-term, ongoing studies, but he did have studies of bear size and health done by pioneers in the field back to 1967, such as Jack Lentfer and, later, Amstrup himself. Amstrup launched new, in-depth fieldwork to take measurements to compare to the old records. The five-year project would track polar bear health and numbers in the southern Beaufort Sea, incorporating data from colleagues on the Canadian side of the border, including from Ian Stirling, who was entering his fourth decade of fieldwork on bears.

Derocher said, "I was out in the field again this last year with Ian. He's in his midsixties, and I hope I'm not doing that when I'm that age. It sounds easy to fly around in a helicopter and catch polar bears, but it's stressful and it's exhausting."

In January 2004, study team members flying over an island north of Prudhoe Bay looking for polar bear dens with an infrared detector saw a trail of blood leading from a collapsed den to a still-fresh carcass of a female bear. A larger bear had smashed the den, crushed the female's skull, and dragged her off for a meal. Later that spring, Stirling followed tracks leading from a den to a female's half-eaten body on the sea ice. Three days later, he saw a large male eating a yearling that it had caught sleeping in a pit in a pressure ridge. For Amstrup and Stirling, with more than twenty and thirty years of studying bears, respectively, the finds were disturbing. Although bears are known to kill other bears, neither had ever seen a bear stalk another polar bear for food. The only mentions of it happening in the scientific literature were when the attacker was starving. Indeed, the living bears Amstrup and Stirling studied in the Beaufort Sea at the time were skinny, and the most obvious reason for their hunger was the long season of ice being far from shore. In 2006, Derocher found another adult female that had been killed for food in similar conditions in the Beaufort.

The findings of the five-year study found that cubs were smaller and less likely to survive the first six months of life than they had been prior to the decline in sea ice before 1990. Adult males in the Beaufort Sea declined in weight from an average of 810 pounds to 725 pounds, and their skulls were smaller—even though they were, on average, older than the bears that were measured before 1990. Margins for error in the old data made it impossible to show a statistically valid decline in polar bear numbers, but the study did establish the declining health of bears on the Arctic coast.

The results from the Beaufort Sea showed a striking parallel to Stirling and Derocher's findings a decade earlier of worsening bear condition in western Hudson Bay. As the climate conditions that had

ABOVE *Autumn, before freeze-up (coastal area, Arctic National Wildlife Refuge). Polar bears are buoyant and well insulated; in calm water, healthy adults may be able to swim up to 100 miles.*

affected bears' health had moved north, bears' decline had moved north too. And it took only ten years. Back in the mid-1990s, the Canadian scientists had predicted that bear numbers in western Hudson Bay would eventually go down. By 2006, that prediction had proved accurate. The western Hudson Bay population was down by 22 percent. If the pattern repeats, as seemed likely, Beaufort Sea bear numbers will go down too.

When I first talked to Steve Amstrup in 2001 and saw the stranded bears at Point Barrow in 2002, no one predicted that changes would come this fast. "Certainly we knew the ice was changing," Amstrup said. "And I knew that when I talked to you in 2001. But we didn't know if that was affecting the population." Now the effect was clear, and what it suggested about the future was not good. While climate scientists disagree whether an ice-free Arctic might come in forty years or a hundred, bears might be gone sooner. Amstrup said ice might have to withdraw from only the continental shelf before polar bears could no longer survive. "As these ice changes are becoming more profound, we might be seeing a threshold where the ice reductions go beyond the point where the bears are able to cope...It's a reasonable hypothesis that at some point the sea ice is just going to be too far offshore for polar bears to make it." At that point, polar bears might disappear.

Schliebe completed his report on polar bear science and traveled to Washington DC to present it to his superiors. Meeting a court-ordered deadline to the day, Secretary of the Interior Dirk Kempthorne announced that the department agreed with Siegel and the Center for Biological Diversity. He proposed listing polar bears as threatened under the Endangered Species Act, telling a news conference, "They are able to live and thrive in one of the world's harshest environments. But there's concern that their habitat may literally be melting."

Environmentalists, including Siegel, who had written the petition, were shocked. The Bush administration remained among the world's last doubters of climate science and had steadfastly resisted

LEFT *Two large male polar bears playing (autumn, coastal plain, Arctic National Wildlife Refuge)*

substantive action to address the problem. Legal experts and politicos debated why Secretary Kempthorne officially recognized the threat to polar bears—potentially giving a powerful legal tool to environmental attorneys who would challenge oil exploration or other development activities the administration supported. They concluded that Kempthorne may not have had a choice. Schliebe's report laid out all the evidence for why polar bears were threatened. If the Interior Department had decided otherwise, Siegel's group could have used that evidence to sue for listing and won. The outcome would be the same, but only after a court fight that could itself be embarrassing to the administration.

Siegel got the public attention she had wanted, and then some. In a way that spiders, corals, and the Kittlitz's murrelet couldn't do, polar bears had become a cultural icon for climate change. "Millions of people now know—cute polar bear cubs are in danger," she said.

Kempthorne's decision began a year-long public process to decide on final listing of the polar bear, which is still in progress as of this writing. Meanwhile, environmental activists have already used the listing process to challenge Arctic oil leasing plans. In the future, any carbon-emitting project that needs a permit from the federal government could be fair game.

A former colleague praised Siegel as a sharp and tireless lawyer, but she used to be an Alaska wilderness guide and she still comes across as perky, even when discussing a dry topic such as environmental litigation. Despite her sunny outlook, however, Siegel couldn't really rejoice over winning for the polar bears, because she was thinking of what was happening in the Arctic.

"Unfortunately, by the time they made the decision, it wasn't future threats anymore. The news has been all so bad. It's just grim and tragic."

She added, however, "I don't think it's too late to save the polar bears."

It's an occupational hazard of those raising environmental alarms to become imprisoned in their own rhetoric. In the case of climate change, activists who sought to overcome political inertia by emphasizing the urgency of the problem now must fight the impression they helped create that the outcome is hopeless. Denial or despair both can destroy the motivation to act. In the Arctic, the climate system itself contributed to a sense of despair that may be misplaced. For reasons scientists don't understand, the climate here oscillates between dramatically different modes of air and sea circulation. The general warming trend of climate change is clear, but it was exaggerated in Alaska's Arctic from 2000 to 2005, when this was the spot with the most anomalous warmth on the globe. In 2006 the pattern seemed to shift and the hot spot moved toward Greenland. Although the Arctic ice pack remained diminished in total, in Alaska temperatures cooled.

The story is complicated, but the moral is simple: we don't know nearly enough to give up on the polar bear. Kassie Siegel has the only reasonable approach: do everything possible, and hope.

PHOTO BY ERIKA HILL

Charles Wohlforth, a lifelong Alaska resident, is the author of several books and numerous magazine articles for publications such as The New Republic, Outside, *and* National Wildlife. *He was the lead reporter on the* Exxon Valdez *oil spill for the* Anchorage Daily News. *He also served on the Anchorage Assembly from 1993 to 1999, representing the downtown area. Wohlforth's most recent book,* The Whale and the Supercomputer: On the Northern Front of Climate Change, *explores Arctic climate change from the perspective of Eskimo whalers and scientific researchers in Barrow, Alaska. It won the Los Angeles Times Book Prize for the best science and technology book in 2005.* Library Journal *also listed it as among the best books of 2004.*

Aquatic Coastal Environment

Wherever they live, animals depend on plants or other animals for food. The images on these pages show parts of the aquatic food web in the Arctic.

TOP ROW, LEFT TO RIGHT *A jellyfish and two types of copepods, which are eaten by bottom feeders such as krill, crabs, small fish, even baleen whales. / Krill, a type of animal plankton, are eaten by seals and whales. / Jellyfish live along the continental shelf. / A hermit crab in its shell on the continental shelf / Small fish live along the continental shelf. / (From top to bottom) Arctic char, cisco, and broad whitefish are fed on by seals, walrus, probably whales, and people.*

BOTTOM ROW, RIGHT TO LEFT *An ivory gull on the pack ice / Walruses are bottom feeders that eat crabs, worms, clams, etc. / Bearded seals, the only bottom-feeding seal, eat crabs and other small life forms. / Bowhead whales, which feed mainly on copepods and krill, are hunted by the Iñupiat. / Polar bears, which hunt ringed and bearded seals, must eat more than 4 pounds of seal fat a day. / Iñupiaq whaler captain Chuck Hopson points to a bowhead whale.*

The polar bear is our keen-eyed sentinel, warning us about the potentially tragic consequences of humanity's overarching effect on the planet.

Daniel Glick

Fever Pitch:
Understanding the Planet's Warming Symptoms

AS PHOTOGRAPHER STEVEN KAZLOWSKI approached a female polar bear until he was close enough to see her teeth, I followed a dozen steps behind, practically chanting words I had learned in Wyoming's grizzly country: You don't have to run faster than the bear. You have to run faster than the person next to you.

Steven, clad in ancient, ragged arctic gear on this wind-torn October day, didn't look as though he'd be hard to outrun. Husky, draped with cameras, and carrying a tripod that could withstand the fierce Beaufort Sea winds, the bearded photographer stood no chance in a race to the pickup. Just to make sure, I maintained a substantial head start.

The bear's apparent nonchalance in the face of our presence made these paranoid preparations unnecessary. For more than an hour, Steven and I stared incredulously as the sow tossed what appeared to be a plastic toy around the frozen Alaskan lagoon. We debated what the "toy" could be, and close inspection through Steven's telephoto lens provided the answer: the polar plaything was a disembodied walrus flipper.

Looking more like a big puppy twirling a cracked Frisbee than the world's largest nonaquatic carnivore whirling a walrus appendage, the white-fleeced sow spent the afternoon tossing her toy around. A spit of land separated her from the Beaufort Sea, where she would soon head to follow the floating offshore sea ice and hunt for seals. Steven and I stared, wild grins on our faces, as the bear threw her walrus Frisbee into a swimming hole, retrieved it, and dove after it again. She repeated the game for at least an hour, as carefree as a golden retriever on a giant grassy field.

Unfortunately, this four-year-old sow has plenty that should

concern her and her kind. Polar bears, which have exquisitely adapted to survive in one of the planet's most inhospitable environments, face a bleak future as their Arctic world heats up. Because of the increasingly indisputable evidence of global warming, the ice that the bears depend on for food and shelter is literally melting under their paws. If current predictions are on target, by the time this sow reaches her twenties, her world will have changed significantly, with less ice, increased competition from brown bears, and prey that has moved farther offshore. The survival of her cubs, grandcubs, and, indeed, her species is increasingly in doubt.

Steven had chosen the polar bear as a visual metaphor to document a region—and its inhabitants—in the throes of immense and rapid transition. The great white bear represents a compelling nudge to the world below the Arctic Circle that there is too much at stake to ignore global warming any longer. The iconic polar bear can be our keen-eyed sentinel, warning us about the potentially tragic consequences of humanity's overarching effect on the planet.

In this, my third trip to Alaska's North Slope in two years, the reality of climate change—and the polar bear's plight—came into sharp focus. My attention had been drawn to the Arctic Circle because scientists have long theorized that warming would happen much faster in the Arctic than in temperate zones. Those theories have now been convincingly confirmed by data that describes a region warming more than twice as fast as lower latitudes.

Even with this widespread scientific agreement about the existence of global warming, the very idea that humans could influence the climate of an entire planet remains almost an imponderable thought to most of us. How in the world do scientists even *know* that the changes we are witnessing are anything out of the ordinary, especially on a planet that has undergone such momentous changes during its 4.6-billion-year history? And even if it might be possible

LEFT *A polar bear tosses an Arctic Frisbee: a walrus flipper (autumn, coastal plain, Arctic National Wildlife Refuge).*

A frequently repeated idea holds that hollow polar bear hairs transmit ultraviolet light to a bear's hide to help it stay warm in the winter. A neat theory—but it turns out to be wrong. Polar bear fur absorbs UV light.

ABOVE *This polar bear played with the flipper on a frozen lagoon for more than an hour.*

RIGHT *Polar bears are curious around humans, often checking out their equipment, such as this tripod and camera (autumn, coastal plain, Arctic National Wildlife Refuge).*

ABOVE *A polar bear and her cub, displaced by grizzly bears from their feeding site, may come back after the grizzlies have left (autumn, coastal plain, Arctic National Wildlife Refuge).*

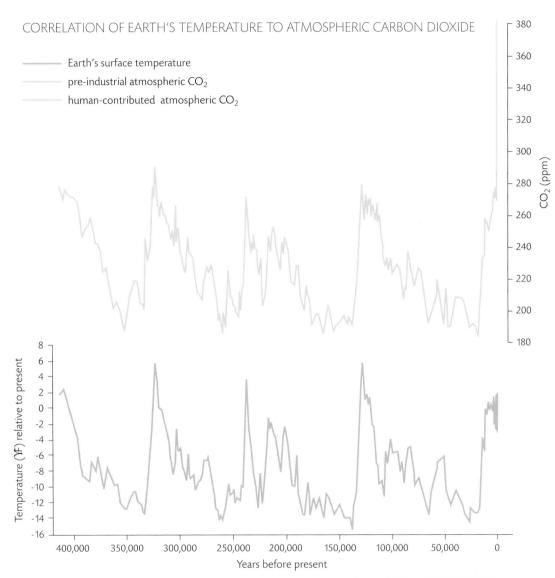

CORRELATION OF EARTH'S TEMPERATURE TO ATMOSPHERIC CARBON DIOXIDE

—— Earth's surface temperature
—— pre-industrial atmospheric CO_2
—— human-contributed atmospheric CO_2

CO_2 (ppm)

Temperature (°F) relative to present

Years before present

Figure 4. By compiling and analyzing a range of paleoclimate (past climate) reconstructions using "proxy" measurements such as ice cores, permafrost boreholes, and calcite on corals, a compelling temperature history emerges.

LEFT *Sow and cub on multiyear ice (summer, Chukchi Sea). Thick rafts of multiyear ice make poor habitat for bears and seals; thinner ice near the edge of the pack harbors most life.*

that human behavior could alter the planet's climate, how would scientists understand the complex systems that govern these things, much less pinpoint *Homo sapiens* as the cause?

What follows is an attempt to answer these fundamental questions. How is the planet changing, and how do we know that it's changing because of anything we're doing?

IT MIGHT HELP TO THINK of the planet as a patient exhibiting some unusual symptoms.

When my daughter complains that she feels sick, I reflexively feel her forehead to see if she's running a fever. In humans, an elevated temperature provides a strong indication that something is amiss: perhaps the presence of a minor bacterial infection that the body will shrug off in a few days; perhaps an emerging worrisome disease.

If her fever persists, I bring my daughter to the doctor, who takes her temperature and vital signs (pulse, respiratory rate, and blood pressure); listens to her heart and lungs; and then peers at her ears, eyes, and throat. Her physician also asks detailed questions—when did the fever start, is it intermittent or constant, does this happen frequently? If it's not immediately clear that my daughter has, say, the flu, her doctor might order a series of tests, such as a detailed workup of blood chemistry. In most cases, this combination of observation, history, and lab results will pinpoint the problem and, hopefully, suggest a course of treatment.

In a tiny number of patients, even this battery of tests will not uncover a fever's cause. In medical terminology, the resulting diagnosis is known as a fever of unknown origin, or FUO.

Consider, then, patient Earth. Scientists who assess the planet's health have been steadily gathering evidence that the planet is getting warmer. Almost every day, these Earth doctors describe more symptoms resulting from this planetary fever. Applying a medical analogy to the condition of our own planet, we might say that Earth has been suffering from an FUO.

As a glance through any medical history book will tell you, scientific breakthroughs often take time to evolve from experimental discovery to common clinical practice. Similarly, the idea that humans could affect global climate is hardly a new one. Swedish Nobel Prize

laureate Svante Arrhenius suggested in 1896 that the earth might heat up due to increased carbon dioxide emissions from coal burning. It took nearly a century, however, for Arrhenius's global warming prediction to enter the popular lexicon. During the heat-wave- and drought-plagued summer of 1988, NASA scientist James Hansen made headlines when he emphatically told a congressional committee that human activity had brought on a planetary fever as surely as a cold causes a stuffy nose.

Hansen's unequivocal interpretation of early global climate data met with skepticism and scorn. But coming just three years after the discovery of the Antarctic ozone hole and its clear association with human-produced chemicals, the assertion that human activity could alter the planet's climate had gained considerable credence. After Hansen's pronouncement, the United Nations convened the Intergovernmental Panel on Climate Change (IPCC), with a far-reaching goal: to consult specialists in every earth science field and give the planet a complete physical examination.

Prior to 1988, scientists had already cataloged elevated global temperatures and increased greenhouse-gas concentrations in the atmosphere. Early computer climate models suggested that this rise in carbon dioxide from fossil-fuel burning, methane from agricultural sources, and other emissions from industrial production would continue to warm the planet as effectively as if we donned a down parka on a hot summer day.

The 1990s further fueled the fever hypothesis. Scientists documented a succession of record-high average annual temperatures and predictable terrestrial responses to warming, like widespread permafrost melting in Arctic regions. Some discounted the warming as inconsequential, akin to a 102-degree Fahrenheit fever that normally accompanies a twenty-four-hour flu bug, while others worried that the symptoms already appeared ominous. One uncontested fact emerged: the earth was measurably changing, in some cases rapidly, with wide-ranging implications for the planet's life-supporting systems.

LEFT *With increasingly warm temperatures, permafrost is no longer permanent—and as it melts, ice cellars, such as this one in Barrow, that are commonly used in some Iñupiat communities may no longer be dependable for food storage year-round.*

ABOVE AND RIGHT *Erosion due to melting permafrost, rising sea levels, and surf along the Arctic coast is causing the land to slump (autumn, above, and summer, at right, Arctic National Wildlife Refuge).*

The FUO raged on, and so did the debate about the fever's origins.

Just as x-rays allow a deeper understanding of human anatomy, twentieth-century advancements in science opened new vistas for researchers who examined the earth itself. The atomic age that unveiled the tiny building blocks of matter incidentally gave scientists a method to pinpoint past climate changes. Ice cores and ancient lake sediments that contain different temperature-sensitive isotopes reveal past temperatures almost as clearly as if they were written on a patient's bedside chart. (Isotopes are atoms of the same element that contain differing numbers of neutrons. Oxygen atoms found in ice, for example, have a distinct atomic weight that reflects the precise temperature when they formed.) Orbiting spacecraft and satellites presented visceral reminders that the Blue Planet's complex processes function without regard to political or even continental boundaries.

By the mid-1990s, a confluence of social and technological forces spawned a scientific revolution arguably as dramatic as the one four centuries earlier, when Copernicus placed the sun, not the earth, at the center of the solar system. Researchers from a slew of new and emerging disciplines began looking at the planet in different ways, as a complex organization of interrelated functions: as an "earth system."

As the twentieth century concluded, humans launched satellites that use infrared spectrometry to examine the earth's extremities, and scientists spelunked into remote caves to study the chemical composition of ancient stalactites. Oceanographers consulted with atmospheric scientists; geochemists parlayed with botanists. Almost everywhere researchers looked, they documented further physical changes to the planet: disappearing glaciers, rising sea level, alterations to atmospheric and oceanic chemistry, earlier and later animal migrations, and changing plant communities. With the advent of the Internet, researchers could share their findings across disciplinary boundaries with the same disregard for national borders exhibited by the planetary climate.

In a familiar irony that often follows in the wake of scientific

LEFT *Walruses and other Arctic carnivores may face increasing competition from warmer-water fish such as halibut (summer, Chukchi Sea).*

discovery, one primary insight gleaned from this new global systems research was the stark realization of how *little* we know: about the gyre of physical, biological, and chemical processes that govern how much carbon dioxide our oceans can absorb; about the role of our most potent greenhouse gas—water vapor (which traps heat from a wide spectrum of the sun's rays)—in modifying cloud cover and weather patterns in a changing world; about the mysteries of the earth's turbulent past climate shifts.

Despite the uncertainty that comes with knowing there is more to learn, scientists now overwhelmingly concur that the cause of the planet's fever can almost certainly be traced to the activities of its dominant species: humans. By clearing large tracts of forest, burning countless BTUs of fossil fuel, and generating megatons of industrial effluent, humans have contributed to the planet's measurable fever.

But how do we feel Earth's forehead to see if it feels warm?

MEDICAL STUDENTS LEARN TO CONDUCT a thorough medical history of a patient when diagnosing an FUO. In analyzing the earth's warming trend, scientists study the planet's past climate to determine whether recent readings constitute part of a natural cycle—or signs of pathology. Taking the temperature of a planet, however, is far more complex than placing a thermometer under a child's tongue.

Humans register core body temperatures very close to 98.6 degrees Fahrenheit (37 degrees Celsius). Although this "normal" temperature fluctuates a little during the course of a day and from person to person, it has probably remained static over time. The earth's climatic history, however, has ridden a thermal roller coaster, experiencing millennia-long ice ages and steamy tropical epochs as well as dramatic seasonal, diurnal (night-and-day), and regional swings.

So how do researchers know the "normal" temperature for patient Earth?

Scientists began systematically measuring planetary temperatures only in the mid-1800s, with the invention of the thermometer. Early readings were taken inconsistently in few places around the globe and at different times of day. Slowly, scientists improved their

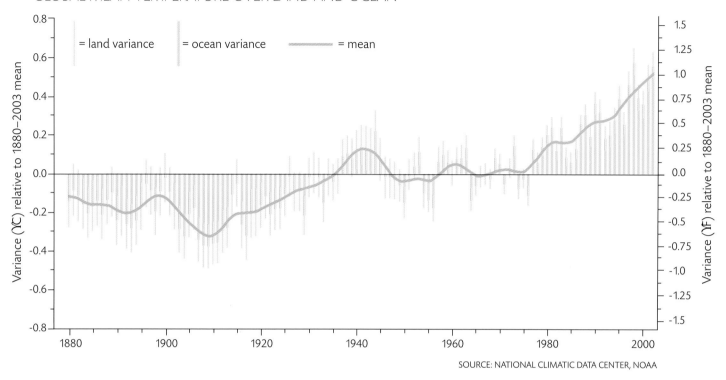

SOURCE: NATIONAL CLIMATIC DATA CENTER, NOAA

Figure 5. During the past century, global surface temperatures have increased at a rate near 1.1°F (0.6°C), but this trend has increased during the past 25 to 30 years to a rate approaching 3.6°F (2°C).

measuring techniques and increased the number and geographical distribution of weather stations. They learned that readings taken near cities were higher than in rural areas (since cities give off their own heat), and they adjusted the data to account for this "urban heat island effect." By the 1950s, many weather stations were moved from inner cities to outlying airports. Researchers ultimately installed stations on all seven continents (there are now more than three thousand worldwide), improved methodology (such as ensuring that readings take place at a uniform time and account for regional daylight-saving-time differences), and calibrated increasingly sensitive instruments in order to compare contemporary readings with the historical record.

Climate scientists also turned to the oceans, realizing that sea captains had measured ocean temperatures since the mid-1800s in order to chart ocean currents. In reviewing historical seafaring observations, more obstacles surfaced: some captains threw canvas or wooden buckets overboard and then stuck a thermometer in the container; after World War II it became customary to take samples from engine intake valves, which provided water from a different ocean depth. These records, too, were painstakingly recalibrated into a useful data set.

Scientists analyzed the combined historical records of both ocean- and land-based measurements, finding surprising agreement. They employed statistical models to discard outlying measurements and averaged huge data sets to eliminate random errors. In its 2007 Fourth Assessment Report, a consensus document collecting

ABOVE *The head of this female polar bear, larger in circumference than her neck, is one characteristic that distinguishes the females from the males (springtime, coastal plain, Arctic National Wildlife Refuge).*

input from more than a thousand scientists and experts worldwide, the IPCC concluded that direct measurements indicated that the earth's average temperature has risen 1.37 degrees Fahrenheit (0.76 degree Celsius) since the nineteenth century. Much of that warming has occurred in the past three decades, and most of it even more recently. According to the 2007 IPCC report, "eleven of the last twelve years (1995–2006) rank among the twelve warmest years in the instrumental record of global surface temperature (since 1850)."

Everyone agrees, however, that 150 years of temperature readings for an ancient planet is inadequate to create a complete medical history. What about reconstructing temperatures that predate the thermometer?

To conduct past climate—or *paleo*climate—reconstructions, scientists use different "proxy" measurements. Past temperature changes are embedded, like a cryptographic code, in the earth's ice, ancient tree rings, corals, lakebed sediments, and even journals written by medieval winemaking friars. By analyzing the isotopic composition of snow in ice cores and the distribution of temperature-sensitive organisms such as diatoms (algae that leave a skeleton made of silica), scientists can tease out what thermal conditions existed before we could directly measure them. Other analyses—such as the precise temperature gradient of deep boreholes in permafrost or the temperature trends revealed by the ratio of different oxygen isotopes of calcite on corals—have aided our understanding of past climate.

Each proxy measurement has its limitations: Tree rings can be found only where soil and climate conditions allowed trees to grow. Corals, conversely, primarily reflect ocean conditions, and ice cores can come only from icy places.

By compiling and analyzing a range of paleoclimate records, a compelling temperature history emerges. Michael Mann of Pennsylvania State University and Phil Jones of the University of East Anglia, using a multiproxy analysis, conclude that the twentieth century was the warmest in the past 1,000 years, and probably in the past 2,000 years. Their published results, controversial at first, have been roundly accepted by their scientific confreres. James Hansen, the NASA scientist who warned Congress about global warming in 1988, published a paper in September 2006 in the *Proceedings of the National Academy of Sciences*, suggesting that the planet is likely as warm as it has been in the past million years.

To learn a little about paleoclimate work, I visited the National Ice Core Laboratory in Lakewood, Colorado, near where I live, where thousands of silver cylindrical containers rest on metal racks inside a vast warehouse maintained at minus 31 degrees Fahrenheit (minus 35 degrees Celsius). Each cylinder contains a frozen ice core, approximately 3 feet long and 5 inches around (1 meter long, 13 centimeters in diameter), drilled from ice sheets in Greenland and Antarctica as well as from glaciers in Washington and Wyoming. Removed from their metallic sheaths, these thick icicles uncannily resemble giant frozen thermometers.

Which is, in a way, exactly what they are. In the eyes of a paleoclimatologist, ice recounts fantastic tales about the earth's climate history: of the rapid cooling of the Younger Dryas era, 12,000 years ago, when arctic flowers bloomed in southern climes; of the Medieval Warming Period, 1,000 years ago, when Norse frontiersman Leif Eriksson helped settle Greenland; of the Little Ice Age that inspired Pieter Brueghel the Elder to paint ice-skaters on frozen Flemish lakes in the mid-1500s.

James White, director of the environmental studies program at the University of Colorado and whose work has helped unlock the mysteries of past rapid climate shifts, showed me an ice core saddled on a light box in the relative warmth of a minus-7.5-degree Fahrenheit (minus-22-degree Celsius) exam room. We stood swaddled in gear suited for an Arctic expedition as White pointed out dark and light "zebra stripes" depicting annual rings in the ice. The alternating layers of dirty compressed snow, sprinkled with the seasonal dust of summer, were interspersed with clearer sections of relatively dust-free winter periods. This one-meter ice core spanned a twenty-year time period around 13,000 years ago.

After we emerged from the frigid room, White explained how the

CLOCKWISE FROM TOP LEFT
A polar bear pulls its head out of a seal breathing hole (Arctic Ocean, near the Arctic Refuge). / Summer, Arctic coast, near the Arctic National Wildlife Refuge / An oil drilling site in the Beaufort Sea, part of Prudhoe Bay's industrial oil fields / Automobile use in the Lower 48 is the source of 28 percent of the United States's greenhouse gas emissions.

ratio of telltale isotope concentrations helps him and his colleagues recognize past climate shifts as confidently as a modern meteorologist can watch a barometer fall and predict a storm moving in. When snow is formed at higher temperatures, for example, it has a higher ratio of oxygen-18 to oxygen-16 isotopes. "Isotopes have been a good paleothermometer," said White.

His study of isotopes from ice cores in Greenland shows that past temperature shifts have been both dramatic and rapid. At the end of the Younger Dryas, parts of the Northern Hemisphere experienced a change in temperature of about 27 degrees Fahrenheit (9 degrees Celsius) in "fifty years or less," White said—perhaps a magnitude similar to a continent moving from Montreal to Miami in the same time span. A key point for White is that, in the past, the earth has experienced rapid warming. But if a similar thing happened in a modern world with 6.6 billion human inhabitants, the effects would be devastating.

When I discuss global warming, the question that seems most to confound people is this: The earth has had ice ages, warming periods, and more ice ages, all before people started burning fossil fuels or dumping greenhouse gases into the atmosphere. Isn't the current warming trend part of a natural cycle?

Well, probably not. It is true that the planet has shifted climatic conditions many times, for various reasons. One of those likely reasons is that during certain epochs, the atmosphere was saturated with carbon dioxide emissions from massive volcanic eruptions or gigantic global fires. Those massive increases in atmospheric carbon dioxide concentrations, from "natural" causes, caused the earth's climate to warm rapidly and completely transformed the planet for thousands of years at a stretch.

The difference is that, today, we are able to measure the same drastic increase in carbon dioxide emissions, but we also know that most of the CO_2 is being emitted by industrial activity. What happened in the past because of "natural" occurrences is now happening largely because of the human penchant to burn carbonized fuels.

WHEN OUR FUO PATIENT has a prolonged fever, the doctor will continue to look for new symptoms. That's because even 1 degree of temperature change can affect a lot of things, if it's the right degree. Think in particular of the difference between 32 and 33 degrees Fahrenheit, temperatures at which H_2O either remains in its solid phase or moves to its liquid state. The variance can mean the difference between an ice cube and a cold glass of water, between snow and rain, between a glacier and a giant alpine puddle. It is the amount the planet has warmed in the past 150 years.

One storied place to look for the difference a degree makes is in Montana's Glacier National Park. The park has become an icon for climate change science, if for no other reason than because people joke that, soon, it will be "the park formerly known as Glacier." Over the past century, photographic surveys have provided the kind of stark, visual, and incontrovertible evidence that confirms a simple truth anybody can understand: when a planet warms, its ice melts.

If Earth is running a fever, then melting glaciers and ice caps might represent the accompanying cold sweat. A twentieth-century global *average* temperature rise is only a tiny part of the story affecting the earth's cryosphere, or icy climes. In many zones where glaciers and ice caps are found, the details of global temperature rise present the real bugaboo: northern latitudes are warming significantly faster than equatorial regions, nighttime temperatures are warming more than daytime temperatures, and winters have warmed twice as fast as summers.

The cumulative effect spells doom for many of the world's glaciers and Arctic ice. Midlatitude glaciers such as those in the western United States are vanishing in a human lifetime. Glacial retreat in the Garhwal Himalayas in India is happening so fast that researchers believe that most central and eastern Himalayan glaciers will virtually disappear by 2035. From the Arctic to Peru, from Switzerland to the equatorial glaciers of Irian Jaya in Indonesia, massive ice caps, monstrous glaciers, and perennial snowfields are shrinking, fast.

Daniel Fagre, a U.S. Geological Survey researcher who has worked extensively in Glacier National Park, applies a medical analogy to his work. "Glacier melt," he says, "is like a blood-panel test for a body's

RIGHT *By the light of the midnight sun, Iñupiaq hunters build an ice ramp for pulling up a bowhead whale (spring, Chukchi Sea).*

physiology; it reflects deeper physiological processes." And the warmer it gets, the faster things melt. This is not good news for glaciers. Unlike species that can migrate in response to environmental change, glaciers "have no adaptive mechanisms," says Fagre. "All they can do is accumulate or lose ice mass in response to the climate."

This problem is accentuated in the Arctic. In the polar bears' world, which is covered in ice and snow for much of the year, most sunlight is reflected back into space. When ice melts earlier in the spring and freezes later in the fall, the landscape fills with larger dark patches of water or vegetation for longer periods, which absorb more light and in turn warm the region further—what scientists call a feedback loop. What that means in lay language is stark and simple: the warmer it gets, the warmer it gets.

According to data compiled in the 2007 IPCC report, evidence of accelerating warming in the Arctic is turning up nearly everyplace scientists look. Thinning ice caps, declining sea ice, earlier ice breakup, and later freeze-up are all documented effects of a warmer Arctic. Greenland's ice cap is shrinking more rapidly than ever, and flow from melting ice and permafrost in northern Russia has increased freshwater concentrations in the Arctic Ocean. As described below, this freshwater flux from melting ice has the potential to disturb ocean circulation and dramatically change world weather in decades—or less.

While the possibility of such abrupt climate change remains theoretical, scientists already know one obvious effect: "Sea level rise," states a 2001 National Academy of Sciences report, "is one of the most apparent and widespread consequences of climate change."

Two obvious things happen when global temperatures increase: more water flows to the seas from melting glaciers and ice caps, and ocean water warms and expands in volume. This combination has raised average global sea level an estimated 6.7 inches (17 centimeters) during the twentieth century, according to the IPCC. Global average sea level continues to rise about 0.05 inch (2 millimeters) per year.

To understand one piece of the sea-level-rise puzzle, scientists turn to an immutable law of physics called thermal expansion. Think of it this way: If you filled a bathtub to the brim and slowly raised the temperature, the bathwater would overflow because its volume would increase with the temperature. For oceans, the equation looks like this: Between 1961 and 2003, the temperature of the top 2,300 feet (700 meters) of the oceans' surface has risen by 0.18 degree Fahrenheit (0.10 degree Celsius), according to the 2007 IPCC report. For every 1.8 degrees Fahrenheit (1 degree Celsius) of temperature rise, seawater expands by a measure of 0.00021. Although the numbers seem minuscule, the impact is significant when multiplied over the unfathomable volume of the world's oceans. The 2007 IPCC report states that thermal expansion alone will likely lead to 1 to 2.6 feet (0.3 to 0.8 meter) of sea level rise over the next two centuries.

Measuring the volume of freshwater added to oceans by melting ice poses a different challenge. Floating icebergs do not alter sea level when they melt any more than a full glass of ice water will overflow when the ice cubes melt. But when an Alaskan glacier on *land* thaws, more water eventually enters the seas. Greenland and Antarctic ice fields represent a huge store of potential freshwater input. The West Antarctic Ice Sheet alone, if it melted, would raise sea level by an estimated 16.4 feet (5 meters).

Some coastal and island communities have already begun implementing evacuation plans due to rising tides. Megacities where human populations have concentrated near coastal plains or river deltas are recognizing their vulnerability: Shanghai, Bangkok, Jakarta, Tokyo, and New York will all be adversely affected by even the most conservative projections of sea level rise. The Netherlands, with half its landmass at or below sea level and significant national wealth, is already engineering for the projected changes. But the predicted political and humanitarian impacts on low-lying, densely populated, and desperately poor countries such as Bangladesh are potentially catastrophic—with global reverberations. In a 2003 report commissioned by the Pentagon, analysts Peter Schwartz and Doug Randall warned that "plausible" climate change scenarios would cause severe disruption in agricultural production due to drought, changing precipitation patterns, and war: "Every time there is a choice between starving and raiding, humans raid," they wrote.

LEFT *Under a full moon at midnight, Iñupiaq whaler Charles Hopson with an* umiak *scans the waters for signs of bowhead whales (spring, Chukchi Sea).*

GREENHOUSE GAS EMISSIONS
United States, 2004

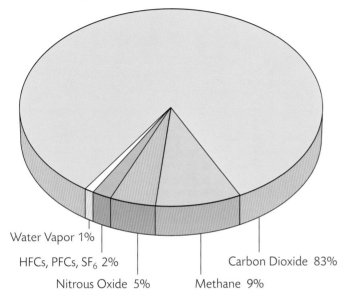

Water Vapor 1%

HFCs, PFCs, SF$_6$ 2%

Nitrous Oxide 5%

Methane 9%

Carbon Dioxide 83%

total emissions = 7.074 BMT CO$_2$E

net emissions (sources + sinks) = 6.204 BMT CO$_2$E

SOURCE: U.S. EPA INVENTORY OF GREENHOUSE GAS EMISSIONS AND SINKS, 2006

Figure 6. In 2004, the United States emitted more than 7 billion metric tons (BMT) of greenhouse gases (CO$_2$E), with carbon dioxide accounting for the largest percentage.

GREENHOUSE GAS BY ECONOMIC SECTOR
United States, 2004

Industry 30%

Transportation 28%

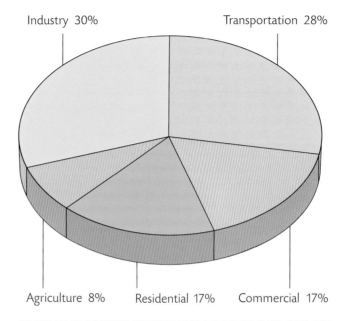

Agriculture 8%

Residential 17%

Commercial 17%

SOURCE: U.S. EPA INVENTORY OF GREENHOUSE GAS EMISSIONS AND SINKS, 2006

Figure 7. Greenhouse gases are emitted by all sectors of the economy; these total emissions have been increasing over time (see Figure 8).

Before actually inundating coastal cities, rising sea level already produces a cascade of effects onshore, including accelerated dune and beach erosion and saltwater intrusion. When salt water enters into freshwater aquifers, it threatens sources of drinking water and makes raising crops problematic. In the Nile delta, where many of Egypt's crops are cultivated, widespread saltwater intrusion would devastate the country's ability to produce food—since Egypt contains little other arable farmland. The current trend in sea level rise is particularly consequential because never before have so many people lived so close to the coasts: an estimated hundred million people live within 3 feet (1 meter) of sea level.

TO RETURN TO OUR MEDICAL SLEUTHING into Earth's FUO, it would be instructive to listen to the patient's chest. The planet's respiratory system has changed dramatically in the past 150 years.

In the late 1950s, a researcher named Charles Keeling began measuring carbon dioxide in the atmosphere from a near-perfect vantage point on Hawaii's 13,678-foot Mauna Loa. The first thing that caught his eye was how carbon dioxide levels rose and fell seasonally. That made sense, since during the spring and summer mass photosynthesis by plants produces oxygen and takes up carbon dioxide. In the fall, plants release carbon dioxide. Keeling's vacillating seasonal curve became famous as a visual representation of the earth "breathing."

Something else about the way the earth was breathing attracted

Keeling's attention. He watched as carbon dioxide levels not only fluctuated seasonally, but also rose year after year. CO_2 levels have climbed from about 315 parts per million (ppm) from his first readings in 1958 to more than 380 ppm today. A primary source for this rise is indisputable: humans' prodigious burning of carbon-laden fossil fuels for their factories, homes, and cars.

Scientists then tackled the problem of gathering CO_2 data that predated Keeling's measurements. Once again, ice cores and other proxies provided answers. Besides being good paleothermometers, ice cores create perfect traps for carbon dioxide locked in air bubbles. The Vostok ice core from Antarctica provides one ancient data set that helped scientists determine that CO_2 levels during the last several hundred thousand years fluctuated between about 200 ppm during ice ages and 275 ppm during the intermittent warm episodes, a level the earth maintained until the Industrial Revolution began. Oil, which fueled the rapid development of the internal combustion engine, pushed CO_2 amounts off the charts.

What happened next was a slow, then a rapid, increase in carbon dioxide levels, matched by increases in other gases associated with industrialization. Pieter Tans, a senior scientist with NOAA's Climate Monitoring and Diagnostics Laboratory, showed me a chart depicting levels of three key greenhouse gases from AD 1000 until the present: carbon dioxide, methane, and nitrous oxide. Humans have contributed to the carbon dioxide rise by burning fossil fuels; to elevated methane levels through power generation, cattle ranching, landfills, and even rice farming; and to nitrous oxide increases from fertilizer use and through motor-vehicle fuel combustion. The charts are almost identical: basically flat until the mid-1800s, when all three gases started an upward trend that turned even more dramatically upward after 1950. "This is what we did," Tans told me, pointing to the parallel spikes. "We have very significantly changed the atmospheric concentration of these gases."

Seen through Tans's eyes, the charts represent a clear lab result pinpointing the cause of our planet's FUO.

That's because Tans and many other atmospheric scientists believe that these gases are collectively at the root of our changing climate. While they compose a small percentage of the earth's

COMPONENTS AND SOURCES OF GREENHOUSE GAS EMISSIONS

The major natural greenhouse gases are water vapor, which causes about 36 to 70 percent of the greenhouse effect on earth (not including clouds); carbon dioxide, which causes 9 to 26 percent; methane, which causes 4 to 9 percent, and ozone, which causes 3 to 7 percent. Note that these do not add up to 100 percent: It is not possible to state that a certain gas causes a certain percentage of the greenhouse effect, because the influences of the various gases are not additive. The higher ends of the percentages are for the gas alone; the lower ends, for the gas counting overlaps. Other greenhouse gases include nitrous oxide, hydrofluorocarbons, perfluorocarbons, chlorofluorocarbons (CFCs), and sulfur hexafluoride (see Figure 6).

Carbon dioxide (CO_2) sources: 82 percent from burning fossil fuels for transportation, industry, and residential and commercial buildings; 2 percent from deforestation, cement products, etc.

Methane sources: landfills, livestock, coal mines, oil and gas operations, agriculture, wastewater treatment, etc.

Nitrous oxide (N_2O) sources: fertilizers, burning of fossil fuels, certain industrial processes, burning forests and crop residues, etc.

Hydrofluorocarbons (HFCs) sources: refrigeration systems; production of industrial, commercial, and consumer products, etc.

Perfluorocarbons (PFCs) sources: refrigeration systems, aluminum production; semiconductor manufacture, electricity production, etc.

Sulfur hexafluoride (SF_6) sources: aluminum smelting, semiconductor manufacture, electric power transmission and distribution equipment, tracer gas for leak detection, etc.

Sources: U.S. Department of Energy's Energy Information Administration; U.S. Environmental Protection Agency; Intergovernmental Panel on Climate Change, First Assessment Report, 1990

TRENDS IN U. S. GREENHOUSE GAS EMISSIONS

SOURCE: U.S. EPA INVENTORY OF U. S. GREENHOUSE
GAS EMISSIONS AND SINKS, 1990–2004

Figure 8. U.S. carbon dioxide emissions (CO$_2$E), expressed here in billions of metric tons (BMT), increased 15.8 percent between 1990 and 2004.

atmosphere, greenhouse gases take what would otherwise be an inhospitably cold orbiting rock and help it remain temperate by orchestrating an intricate dance between the reflection of the sun's radiation by the earth back to space (cooling the earth) and the absorption of radiation in the atmosphere (trapping radiation at the surface and thus warming the earth). Unfortunately, too much of even a good thing can be a problem, with greenhouse gases as with sunbathing. "This is a climate change driver," said Tans, poking the graphs definitively with his index finger.

In 1896 Svante Arrhenius wondered if "the mean temperature of the ground [is] in any way influenced by the presence of heat-absorbing gases in the atmosphere?" Tans is convinced that the answer is unequivocal. "We know the radiative properties of these gases," he said. "It is inconceivable to me that it would not have a significant effect."

IF THE EARTH'S ATMOSPHERE is analogous to a respiratory system, the world's oceans can be considered the planet's circulatory system.

Oceans compose more than 70 percent of our planet's surface and account for 96 percent of the earth's water, yet ocean processes remain among the most uncharted and poorly understood of the earth's systems. It wasn't until the ten-year-long World Ocean Circulation Experiment launched in 1990 that researchers began to formulate a clear description of what is now called the ocean conveyor belt.

Oceans, in effect, mimic some functions of the human circulatory system. Just as arteries carry oxygenated blood from the heart to the extremities, and veins return blood to be replenished with oxygen, oceans provide life-sustaining circulation to the planet. Driven by a combination of temperature, salinity, and prevailing winds, ocean currents are critical in cooling, warming, and watering the planet's terrestrial surfaces—and especially in transferring heat from the equator to the poles.

The "engine" for this circulation is the thermohaline current (*thermo* for temperature and *haline* for salinity). As ocean conveyor belts such as the Gulf Stream carry seawater from warm, saltier, low-latitude waters, these warm currents meet colder, less salty water at the poles—which is also denser. The denser water sinks deep into the ocean, recirculating over long periods back toward the equator. "If you can't understand the circulation, you can't understand how the parts of the body are connected," says John Woods, a professor of oceanography at the United Kingdom's Imperial College.

As scientists began to understand those connections, however, they also documented that the ocean's waters were becoming warmer, less saline, and more acidic as a consequence of increased atmospheric temperatures and carbon dioxide levels. While ocean temperatures are rising at only half the rate of atmospheric temperatures, the oceanic temperature changes are in many ways more profound. Since water is a thousand times denser than air, even small perturbations in sea temperatures may have disproportionately stronger effects on ocean systems. (By way of contrast, meteorologists measure air temperature to the nearest degree. Oceanographers

ABOVE *Summertime, Arctic Ocean*

measure ocean temperature to the hundredth of a degree.)

In addition to ocean temperatures rising, the ratio of freshwater to salt water is changing, especially near the poles where glaciers and ice are melting so fast, spilling freshwater into polar seas. "The largest and most dramatic oceanic change ever measured in the era of modern instruments" is the changing salinity of the subpolar seas bordering the North Atlantic, says Robert Gagosian, past president and director of the Woods Hole Oceanographic Institution.

Gagosian believes that oceans hold the key to potential significant future shifts in the earth's climate. "Scientists have so far identified only one viable mechanism to induce large, global, abrupt climate changes: a swift reorganization of the ocean currents circulating around the earth," he says. He warns that too much change in ocean temperature and salinity could bring the engine that drives the thermohaline current grinding to a halt.

The potential reorganization of thermohaline currents remains a disturbing, if unproven, theory. But the link between changing atmospheric chemistry and its effect on oceans is indisputable, says Joanie Kleypas, a marine ecologist at the National Center for Atmospheric Research. She and others have documented that the oceans are important carbon dioxide "sinks," or absorption centers, that take up about a third of the CO_2 released into the atmosphere. Data from the various monitoring programs show that CO_2 levels at the ocean surface are rising at about the same rate as atmospheric CO_2, leading to a critical change in ocean chemistry.

Too much CO_2 in the oceans could be the catalyst for cascading ecological shifts, says Kleypas. She and her colleagues released a report in 2006 that detailed how oceans were manifesting the most dramatic changes in marine chemistry in the past 650,000 years. As atmospheric carbon dioxide dissolves in the ocean, it becomes carbonic acid and raises the pH. "It's like adding acid to the ocean," she says. Kleypas worries, among other things, about the effect of this relatively rapid change on marine life. "Corals have never seen seawater chemistry like this," she says. "Animals have not evolved in that pH. It's outside of their range."

LEFT *A cub swimming in ice water*

That challenge of accelerated evolutionary pressure summarizes the problem facing many animals and plants in a world that is warming as fast as ours. Certain flora and fauna will undoubtedly benefit from the effects of climate change and may be able to expand their range into previously inhospitable habitat. But for creatures at the edge, the only place to go may be into memory.

AFTER 110 YEARS OF SLEUTHING since Svante Arrhenius first raised the possibility of human-driven climate change, the cause of our planetary fever no longer remains a complete mystery. The University of Colorado's James White offers a definitive diagnosis. "It's not an FUO anymore," White says. "You can't argue with the basic fact that we're changing the planet." The 2007 IPCC Fourth Assessment Report, which represents the culmination of decades-long examination of the planet's fever symptoms, concludes emphatically that humans are almost certainly at the root of the planetary fever.

For polar bears, who live on an ice edge that is disappearing, few of these climate changes bode well. Despite the playful behavior of the sow we watched, Steven Kazlowski and I couldn't help but share a sobering moment as we sat safely in the truck after the sun crouched below the horizon. He marveled at the intricate web of life he had discovered in this frankly desolate place, from the bearded seals to the Iñupiaq whalers, from the globetrotting Arctic terns to the 10-pound polar bear cubs that would have to survive in a world substantially different from their mother's. He wondered aloud, and I nodded agreement, what it would take for people to take notice and actually change their behavior.

I broke the ensuing silence with a joke about staying a few steps behind him while we were outside the truck. "You can't run faster than the bear," he said.

Unfortunately, I thought, the bear might not be able to run fast enough to outrun us, either.

Daniel Glick is the author of Monkey Dancing: A Father, Two Kids, and a Journey to the Ends of the Earth, *a Colorado Book Award–winning account of a trip he took with his son and daughter to places of great ecological wonder that are threatened by human development. A correspondent for* Newsweek *for thirteen years, Glick co-authored the 2004* National Geographic *cover story entitled "Global Warning: Bulletins from a Warmer World" that won an Overseas Press Club award. He has written for numerous other magazines, including* Smithsonian, Outside, Rolling Stone, *the* Washington Post Magazine, *and* Harpers. *Glick also wrote* Powder Burn: Arson, Money and Mystery on Vail Mountain, *an investigation into the most infamous act of ecoterrorism in U.S. history. In 2001, he was awarded a Ted Scripps Fellowship at the University of Colorado, one of five journalists chosen annually to spend an academic year researching environmental law, policy, and science. In 2006, he spent four months as a Knight International Journalism Fellow in Algeria with his two children.*

Steven Kazlowski

THE POLAR BEAR AND THE ARCTIC FOX

IN LATE AUTUMN ALONG THE CHUKCHI *and Beaufort seas, the warming cycle of summer ends and the familiar, crisp scent of snow returns to the air. Multiyear ice that pulled away from the coast in the spring slowly inches closer to the land as the temperature continues to drop. And on the tawny sand beaches that rim these northern seas, an occasional Arctic fox can be seen, sometimes still and silent, sometimes pacing along the water's edge, but always looking out to sea, waiting for the ice.*

The transition of one season into another is often accompanied by shifts in behavior of the animals that thrive in this unique habitat. Northern migrations in spring become southern migrations in fall. Active feeding and rearing of offspring taper off, and, for some creatures, shorter daylight hours trigger hibernation patterns. For others, these changes are merely a signal to begin a new phase in the never-ending cycle of life. The Arctic fox is one of those rare mammals whose coat changes with the seasons, turning from its dark gray or warm brown summer fur to snowy white in winter. This dramatic transformation heralds another change for the small fox: in summer, its habitat is the inland Arctic tundra, near the edge of the boreal forest, but late in the year it instinctively moves toward the coast. Quickly autumn ends, and the temperature plummets again overnight. And even though the calendar says otherwise, in these parts winter has arrived.

The ice is so close to the land now that you can hear the sound of the water softly lapping against it. There might be perhaps half a dozen foxes on a single stretch of beach, exhibiting signs of anxiety or anticipation as they pace and whine along the shore. And then, instinctively, they know it's time: almost as one, the foxes leap for the ice, across the treacherous gap of freezing water that will soon close up, scrambling to maintain their footing on the hard landing. Then each one stops for a moment and

sniffs the air, as if searching the distance for some unnamed joy. The long night of winter has fallen, and the foxes, having made the leap, trot off into the darkness, into the land of ice.

—based on anecdotes by Iñupiaq elder Arnold Brower Sr.,
as told to editor Christine Clifton-Thornton

Sometime in April, as the Arctic ice starts to open up in the form of leads, the bowhead whales begin their annual spring migration along Alaska's northwestern coast. There, they feed on the nutrient-rich krill and zooplankton, a necessary precursor to their calving that takes place between April and early June.

In the Iñupiaq village of Barrow, Alaska, there are more than fifty whaling crews, each made up of family members and friends. Although the crews are convivial and known for their generosity toward one another, whaling is serious business. This particular spring, I was with the Hopson I whaling crew, around ten people altogether, but usually just a few—three to seven—go out at a time; we were driving snow machines toward the edge of the lead. A lead indicates open water, where whales get their air, and the animals generally like to swim at the edge much of the time. But for us, reaching a lead is no small task. Leads can open up in various places, and it takes anywhere from a few days to several weeks to get to one, depending on ice conditions and on the number of people and how hard they work. I was with a slow-moving group in difficult ice conditions, so it had taken us more than a week to reach this lead, having slowly cut our way through the massive blockage of pressure ridges and jumbled ice in our path.

During spring whaling, whaling crews camp on the edge of an open lead, waiting for just the right-sized bowhead whale to pass by. Crews construct a wind blind to wait in, and one crew member always sits toward the front of the wind blind on the ice, on the lookout and ready to go. There's a lot of down time. When a whale is

LEFT *Late autumn, coastal plain, Arctic National Wildlife Refuge*

ABOVE *An Arctic fox leaps high in the air as it hunts rodents.*

CLOCKWISE FROM TOP LEFT
A polar bear sniffs the wind, perhaps warned by the bark of an Arctic fox that danger is nearby. / Seal remains and blood on the ice are all a hungry polar bear leaves behind at a seal breathing hole. / An Arctic fox in its full winter coat / In winter, Arctic foxes (this one not yet in its full summer coat) can sometimes be seen traveling close behind polar bears, which typically eat only a seal's blubber, leaving the meat for the fox to scavenge.

LEFT *Iñupiaq whaler Stacey Hopson on the frozen Chukchi Sea (spring, Point Barrow, Alaska)*

RIGHT *A whaling camp on safe shorefast ice during spring whaling season waiting for the right conditions to go back out to the lead (Chukchi Sea).*

finally chosen, the crew harpoons it from either the edge of the ice or from an *umiak* (bearded seal–skin boat). Because of dangerous ice conditions, the challenge is to stay on the edge of the lead and out of the water.

We were camped on a flat pan of multiyear freshwater ice, surround by jumbled ice. Flat pans of ice are generally the safest spot to be if the lead closes. The problem with a lead closing is that freshwater ice (unlike saltwater ice, which bends) can crumble right beneath your feet as ice from the other side of the lead closes in and puts pressure against the pan. The day after we reached the edge of the lead, it started to close up, so we had to move camp. We packed up and moved several pressure ridges in toward shore to get on safer, more stable ice. Because the ice is so changeable, sometimes you have to move camp two or three times a day to be safe—an exhausting chore.

The next day we went back to the lead's edge to check conditions of the lead and of the ice at the lead's edge. Twenty feet of the pan had broken up into boulder-sized ice chunks, now floating in the sea. The trick about being on the ice is that you have to be on your guard at all times. If you don't make the effort, instead of waking up in your tent one morning, you could be one of those ice chunks in the water.

As we examined what had become of our previous campsite and looked at what was going on near the lead, we came across fresh polar bear tracks. This was no great surprise: polar bears typically walk the edge of the leads, hunting for seals. But then we also saw a trail of fresh Arctic fox tracks. Arctic foxes usually head back to land for mating season in March and April. It looked as if the two had passed us by, out of our line of sight. I tried not to show my disappointment; I would have loved to get some photos of the bear and the fox, not just their tracks.

A little while later, we heard an Arctic fox bark. I was sure it was a warning bark: the fox was signaling that we'd invaded its space.

We started heading back to camp—and then, suddenly, we met up with a polar bear. It was big, and it was running away from where we were. One of the whaling crew members wanted to shoot it, so he started chasing it, and we all followed, trotting after him across the ice. Luckily for the bear, it made it safely onto rough ice; the crewman hesitated once or twice and didn't manage to make a shot.

While I tried to piece together what was going on, my friends told me stories of the close tie between polar bears and Arctic foxes, stories told to them by friends and family, some passed down by ancestors. This relationship is not a myth; the Iñupiat have observed it for countless years. The bond may appear to be cooperative—polar bears kill seals and usually eat only the fat, while the foxes eat the meat the bears leave behind—but rarely does one beast do something for another without motivation or reciprocity.

But what could a fox give a polar bear in return for its meal? Maybe companionship; maybe an extra set of eyes and ears to warn the polar bear of approaching danger. Observed fox-and-bear interactions include an apparently teasing behavior, in which the small white fox chases and nips at the massive white bear, even playfully leaping onto its back while the bear continues to lumber along.

Listening to the fox barking now, we concluded that it was warning the polar bear of our presence, and the polar bear was doubling back around us to get away. This seemed quite obvious to me, though scientists might disagree. Who's to say that certain Arctic foxes and certain polar bears do not have special relationships in which they get along as friends? My disappointment vanished. This bear and fox clearly had been walking the ice edge together.

Christine Clifton-Thornton

SPRING WHALING: A CONVERSATION WITH ARNOLD BROWER SR.

MY QUEST TO PHOTOGRAPH POLAR BEARS in the Arctic natu-rally led me to introduce myself to the communities of Iñupiat, who know these lands best. I was very fortunate; my new friends welcomed me into their midst, and I found myself with numerous opportunities to photo-graph aspects of their lives, which amazes me even now.

In mid-May, during the spring whaling season, I had been on and off the ice outside of Barrow, Alaska, trying to photograph wildlife for four weeks. We were having a stretch of good weather—clear skies, light winds, temperatures of 0 to minus 5 degrees Fahrenheit at night and 10 to 15 degrees Fahrenheit during the day. I was staying with Chuck Hop-son's whaling crew and had been sleeping during the day, since the nicest light for photography was in the evening. On this day, I awoke around 4:00 PM to the sound of Perry Hopson's snow machine racing up to the camp. Arnold Brower's crew—the ABC crew—had gotten a bowhead whale, and Perry was grabbing a sled to carry the Hopson I crew's shares of the whale after they helped butchered it. I asked if I could follow along, and he agreed. We took off from camp and picked up crew member Cur-tis Hopson in town, and then the three of us headed back out on the ice to the ABC crew's camp. When we arrived, people were showing up from other crews and from town to help butcher the whale.

Perry and Curtis introduced me to a few people and told them what I was doing, and I introduced myself to others as I took pictures of folks, also gathering names and addresses so I could send them photographs. I stayed there all night, leaving at 10:00 AM the next morning. At mid-night the following evening, they were still finishing up.

Several things about photographing this particular whale made the experience special, beginning with the whale's immense size and the opti-mal weather conditions. We had sunset light all night, with no fog, which *makes for the most dramatic pictures: two-dimensional photographs end up seeming three-dimensional instead. It was also an amazing chance to witness how the Iñupiaq community comes together as a whole to harvest a gift from the sea. Editor Christine Clifton-Thornton interviewed Arnold Brower Sr., captain of the ABC crew, in his home just days later.*

—Steven Kazlowski

Arnold Brower Sr. talks often of learning. The soft-spoken father of seventeen, a revered Iñupiaq Eskimo elder, sits in an easy chair in his living room in Barrow, sipping a cup of Lipton tea. Born in this village of now nearly five thousand residents back when the popula-tion barely reached double digits, he discusses the community with the intimacy of a lifelong resident. Throughout the evening, family members drop by—a common occurrence here—and help themselves to tea and conversation. In the background, the CB radio chatters as another successful whale hunt is celebrated in the village. Brower is warm and animated, imparting a sense of wonder and happiness usually found only in young children. He laughs often, with his whole body, his head thrown back, his bright eyes twinkling.

Brower talks about his experiences and his community with the ease of one who is often consulted on such matters. He tells of his years in the reindeer service, starting at age fifteen, when he tended the herds belonging to his mother's family and first learned the ways of the land. He talks about his lifetime of hunting—polar bears, foxes, caribou, seals, whales—and the connections he sees between the animals and the seasons, the ice and the land. And he talks about his experiences in World War II, when he served with William Egan, who later became Alaska's first governor and appointed Brower to the board of the Alaska Department of Fish and Game. Brower occasion-ally loses his train of thought as he reminisces about his beloved wife of fifty years, who passed away in 2000; he compares her gentleways

ABOVE   *Iñupiaq elder Arnold Brower Sr.*

LEFT   *Bowhead whales feed on krill and zooplankton (summer, Chukchi Sea).*

ABOVE *Harpooning a bowhead whale*

CLOCKWISE FROM TOP LEFT
Iñupiaq whalers of the Hopson I crew and their families pray together before heading out for the spring hunt (Barrow, Alaska). The ancient whaling tradition remains vital to the community's culture and economy. / Wearing a polar bear ruff, a whaler scouts the water for bowhead whales (Chukchi Sea). / Whalers make a hole in the pack ice so animals—maybe a beluga whale—can emerge (spring, Chukchi Sea). / Protected from the wind by a canvas blind, a spring whaling crew takes turns watching for bowhead whales.

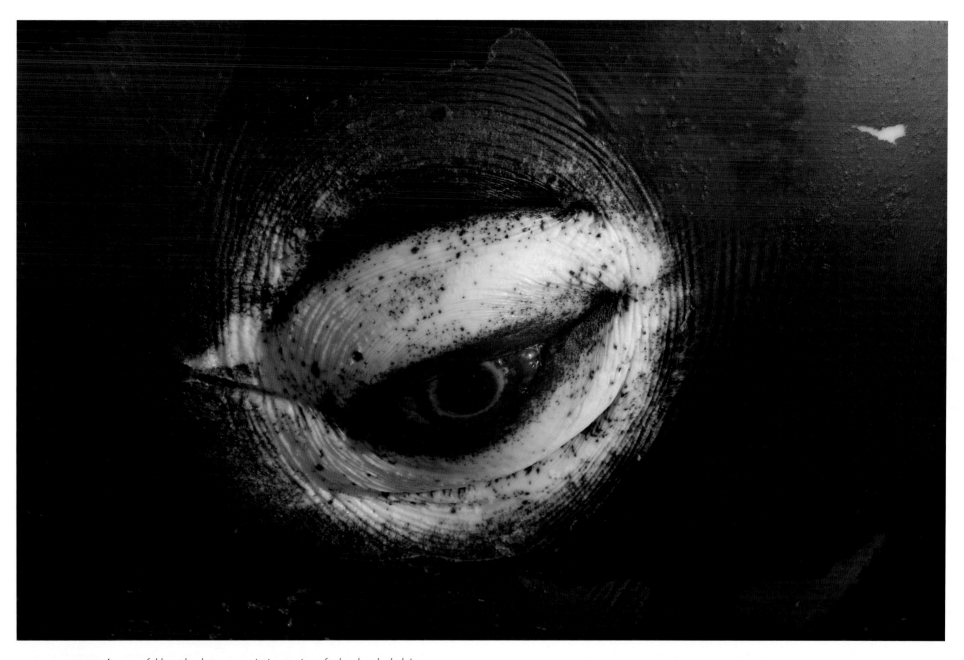

ABOVE *A successful hunt leads to a rare, intimate view of a bowhead whale's eye.*

CLOCKWISE FROM TOP LEFT
The ABC crew, with the help of the whole community, pulls the immense whale onto shore, where they will butcher it and share the meat with everyone. / At 3:00 AM, Ned Arey points to an old wound discovered in the harvested whale, which contained a New England whaling harpoon head later dated to 1878. / Whalers (or hookers, as they're called) pulling–hooking–long strips of muktuk (whale skin and blubber) / Dividing shares of the whale meat for the community

to those of the golden plover. Amid his stories, his conversation inevitably returns to education. "I hardly learned anything else except hunting, how to follow the seasons and the animals," he says quietly. "I didn't have much schooling, but I understand it and wanted my children to go. I learned a lot from my parents, and I continue to learn from my children."

He becomes more expressive when talking about whaling. The spring whaling season is in full swing, and the excitement in the village over recent whaling successes is palpable. "Whaling draws us together as a community," says Brower. "You have to have teamwork to be a whaling team. And we share what we get. Sharing is a product of the tribe. That's how we survive, I guess. Subsistence is the lifestyle here; you can't take it away."

The whales themselves are marked with the Iñupiaq Eskimos' subsistence history. Each hunt inevitably yields a whale whose body holds scars and even ancient harpoon heads of whaling seasons long past. The life span of bowhead whales is difficult to determine, but they are thought to live for more than 100 years. The 48-foot, 8-inch whale brought in this spring by Arnold's ABC crew was imbedded with a kind of whaling bomb used by Yankee whalers in the 1800s, which Brower immediately sent out for study. The artifact was dated to around 1878.

But the Iñupiaq subsistence lifestyle is changing—because the land itself is changing. "The ice is not the same as it used to be. The old ice that used to pile up and anchor out there," Brower says, pointing to the sea that's visible through the window, "is missing. It's disappearing. There is more water than ice now, and the land beneath it is eroding away." There is no scientific equivocation in Brower's words; he states this as fact. He doesn't need anyone else to tell him about the changes in the climate; he has been watching this land for eighty-five years. "We live with it," he says simply.

"When you have a subsistence lifestyle, you have to hustle like mad to survive months of winter. In 1948 I made my hunting camp a hundred miles from here. We dug cellars into the permafrost; that's where we keep the food cold. We have these cellars in town, too. You sometimes work without sleeping to keep your cellar full.

"Now I go out there and hunt, but my cellar," he shakes his head in disbelief, "has water in it. The permafrost is melting. It used to be pure ice, but ten years ago I started to see water. All that time before, it never did happen."

The missing ice makes it harder to hunt the animals his community needs to survive. But the hunters, too, are missing: more and more of his people are leaving the village for life in the cities. Brower believes the ice, the animals, and the Iñupiat are tied together; if one disappears, the others might, too.

"Here's my question," he says. "What's really happening? Something is wrong." He pauses. Then he nods; he knows the answer. He is a revered wise man, after all. "Maybe the whole world is sick."

Brower believes education can help reverse some of these changes. He does his part to pass on the traditions of his people's subsistence existence by teaching youngsters how to hunt, how to make fishing nets—the old ways he has cultivated all his life—even though fewer and fewer of the village's children arrive at his door each year, eager to learn. "How do we preserve the polar bear and the whale now that the ice is going away?" Brower wonders aloud.

CLOCKWISE FROM TOP LEFT
Iñupiaq whaler Curtis Hopson, in a beaver hat, and Yupiq whaler Waska Williams Jr., in a wolverine ruff / The end of a long day / An Iñupiaq woman is tossed into the air during Nalukatuk (Blanket Toss), a traditional celebration of the whaling season. / A nearly white ice rainbow

Just how closely intertwined are the lives of the Iñupiat and the polar bear, two crafty, sharp-witted, keenly observant Arctic predators?

Richard Nelson

Hunting Wisdom: The Iñupiat and the Polar Bear

"I WAS WALKING BY MYSELF WAY OUT on the pack ice...and all of a sudden, on the far side of a big flat place—I saw a polar bear."

The old man peered at the endless, ice-covered Arctic Ocean. He was lean, bright eyed, still active in his midseventies, and everyone said he was the greatest Iñupiaq Eskimo hunter. He possessed a singular and mystifying genius, as if he could project himself into an animal's mind. I could feel it especially when he told of his encounters with *nanuq*—the polar bear.

"I had no place to hide on that flat ice," he recalled. "And I knew the bear would see my dark parka from far away. So I couldn't get any closer to him."

A subtle, confident smile crossed the man's face as he remembered what happened next.

"I laid down on the ice, sideways to the bear, so he'd see something long and dark, and I started acting like a seal that comes up through a crack to sleep on the ice."

He paused for a long moment to fasten my attention, as he often did when he had something important to say.

"I wanted that bear to hunt me.

"Every once in a while, I lifted my head really quick, like a seal looking around to make sure there's no danger. Then I put my head back down, same as a seal when it starts sleeping again.

"Pretty soon I saw the bear crawling toward me, really slow—hunting that little seal, he thinks. Every few minutes I jerked my head up and he stopped. When my head went down, he'd sneak again."

There was no hint of recollected fear in the old man's voice, nor was there a trace of bluster or bravado.

"That bear kept coming closer and closer. Pretty soon he'll run at me, the way polar bears always do when they kill a seal. But I had my rifle ready.

"I waited 'til he got really close. And by the time I shot, I knew there's no way to miss. That's how I got the bear."

He smiled openly now, plainly, straightforwardly proud—not of what he was but of who he was—an Iñupiaq hunter who embodied the craft and brilliance of his people.

BLOOD TRAILS

I had many chances to hear the old man's stories during a year I spent with Iñupiaq people, helping to record their hunting ways, their knowledge of sea ice, and their strategies for survival in one of earth's most challenging environments. As a young graduate student in anthropology during the mid-1960s, I was sponsored by the U.S. Air Force to gather this information, which would be incorporated into pilots' polar survival manuals. This work acknowledged something that was long overdue: that indigenous people like the Iñupiat have much to teach us about the world.

The villagers generously allowed me to become an apprentice, recognizing that I would have to learn their hunting and survival skills myself in order to fully and accurately describe them. They must have been amused by the prospect. I had never hunted in my life, had never seen the frozen polar sea, had never driven a dog team, had never imagined encountering walruses, bowhead whales, or caribou in the wilds of Arctic Alaska. And I had certainly never thought of placing my footsteps in the tracks of a polar bear.

On my first seal hunt, I ventured several miles out on the early winter ice with an Iñupiaq hunter. The temperature was far below zero, the intensely cold snow crackled under our boots, and we found a wide fissure—or lead—with dense clouds of steam rising from

LEFT *The blubber-rich* natchiq *(ringed seal), which weighs about 150 pounds, is a polar bear's favorite prey (spring, Chukchi Sea).*

LEFT *The ringed seal's* allu *(breathing hole) is a narrow, vertical tunnel through ice that may be more than 10 feet thick; here, this hole for hauling out of the water is in ice about 6 inches thick (springtime, Chukchi Sea).*

RIGHT *Geoff Carroll and Marie Adams dogsled for recreation (springtime, Chukchi Sea). Snowmobiles have replaced dogsled teams as the preferred mode of transportation for Iñupiaq hunters.*

ABOVE *A polar bear hunts a young bearded seal (summer, Arctic Ocean).*

ABOVE *Polar bears kill beluga whales at any chance, several times a year. When a beluga gets stuck in the ice at a breathing hole, a bear will take advantage of the opportunity for a kill (spring, Chukchi Sea).*

the black water. We stood near the ice edge with our rifles, watching for seals that might bob up nearby.

"If you're lucky enough to get a *natchiq*—a ringed seal," my companion advised, "you can use a shoulder harness to drag it back to the village. The dead seal leaves a trail of blood on the ice, and if a hungry polar bear comes along, it might follow that blood toward the village, even right up to the houses. People are always watching... and sometimes they get a polar bear that way.

"But the old hunters tell us never to forget: If you're dragging a seal on the ice and all of a sudden you feel something pull on it, don't even look to see what's happening. Just drop that shoulder harness and get your rifle ready, because it might be a polar bear grabbing your seal."

At the time, I couldn't fathom the shock of facing such a massive and imposing creature. What would it feel like, I wondered, to stare directly into the eyes of a polar bear?

I wouldn't find out until forty years later, when I did exactly that— but under very different circumstances.

ENCOUNTER

It happened in October 2005, beside a heap of moldering whale bones on the Beaufort Sea coast, at the edge of the Arctic National Wildlife Refuge. I was caught in the gaze of a hulking female polar bear that was flanked by her two half-grown cubs. At first the mother bear seemed entirely too interested in my presence, although I kept a safe and respectful distance. She lowered her head, licked her bloodstained lips, and craned her serpentine neck back and forth, as if deciding what to do next.

Then one of the cubs let out a high-pitched bawling yowl, as it had done several times over the past hour during squabbles with its sibling over bits of food. This time, however, the cub was staring away from me, toward an ice-covered lagoon that stretched out beyond the bears. I immediately saw why. A huge male bear loomed like an apparition though the veils of blowing snow, and I had instantly become irrelevant.

The male shambled circuitously toward the whale bones where the mother and her cubs had been scavenging. As he came closer, I was awed by the breadth of his back, the mass of his shoulders and haunches, and—above all—by the size of his paws. Great and thick and splayed, they looked wider than a basketball, as pure white as the rest of him except for the five polished ebony claws.

The cubs took refuge behind their mother, and she wasted no time letting the male know he wasn't welcome. Although she was much smaller than the prodigiously muscled intruder, you couldn't miss her unfazed, unmodulated aggression. Jaw to jaw, the two bears met in a cacophony of growls that sounded like lions in full battle. The cubs paced at their mother's heels, seemingly torn between the urge to run and the imperative to stay within her protection.

After a protracted but bloodless confrontation, it was the male who grudgingly backed off, shifting his gaze between the mother bear, the whale bones she defended, and the easy option of retreating onto the ice. Finally he zigzagged away, pausing at intervals to peer back. I noticed that his inward-turning forepaws left pigeon-toed tracks on the snow. Despite his ponderous size, the bear moved with an easy, effortless, almost balletic grace. It was hard to comprehend that such power could be so perfectly contained.

Across the half-mile-wide lagoon there was a sandy barrier island where this male and others like him spent most of the daylight hours sleeping among the snowdrifts. Glassing carefully with binoculars, I could sometimes pick out ten or more of them. They usually waited until nightfall and then came in to take contentious ownership of the carrion. Their growls and bellows rolled away beneath the bright, quavering bands of aurora.

When the visibility wasn't curtailed by blowing snow, I could see dark water and careening surf out beyond the barrier island. Winter had scarcely begun, and the great polar ice pack was far out beyond the horizon. These bears had spent their summer months on the distant, drifting floes, but with the onset of colder weather they began swimming shoreward, attracted by the scent of carrion or drawn by a memory of scavenging here during previous years.

For several hours, the mother bear and her two cubs ripped at the bones and argued with competitors who edged in to feed nearby.

BEACHCOMBING

When I lived in Wainwright, Alaska, forty years ago, Iñupiaq villagers often hunted for polar bears in the fall, when the animals came ashore to feed on the beached remains of walruses, seals, and whales that had died of various causes during the previous months. This may have been the most productive season for polar bear hunting. Men traveled by dog team and camped along the snow-covered shores, hoping to encounter the big animals. Usually these were solitary bears, but occasionally they gathered in small groups to gnaw at the meat, fat, and gristle. According to the elders, polar bears would do this for a few weeks, until early winter storms pushed the pack ice in against the land, and then they would be gone almost overnight, wandering off to spend the winter hunting seals that live beneath the ice. However important this hunting may have been for Iñupiaq people, biologists point out that the majority of polar bears stay out on the ice, well away from shore, through the fall season.

In recent years, polar bears have also been attracted by the scraps and bones of bowhead whales taken just before freeze-up by Iñupiaq subsistence hunters. The ancient whaling tradition remains vital to the culture and economy of these remote communities. Modern technology has made the whale hunt more humane and efficient, so that smaller numbers of animals are taken to satisfy the villagers' need for food. In earlier times, remnants from the whales were hauled back out to deep water, but nowadays they may be left onshore. As the Arctic climate grows warmer and the sea ice diminishes, it is interesting to speculate on the possibility that local, opportunistic food sources like this might become more important for some polar bears.

During the 1960s, Iñupiaq hunters would travel by dog team along the freshly snow-covered shores each fall, looking for bears. Men who found beached carrion sometimes made a camp, tethering their sled dogs close by. Inside nothing more than flimsy canvas walls, the Iñupiaq hunters seemed completely unintimidated by the prospect of a midnight visitor. They slept lightly, rifles at hand, listening for the chorus of barks and howls that would warn of a bear's approach.

Once, traveling alone by dog team, I came across a walrus

carcass—frozen so hard I could scarcely mark it with my ax—yet a polar bear had gnawed deep gashes in the hide and had torn flesh from the exposed bones. The bear's tracks meandered off onto the ice pack, but over the following weeks hunters went there again and again, hoping another would return.

Back then, any hunter lucky enough to take a polar bear could sell the hide for a good sum, but the commercial market ended with the 1972 U.S. Marine Mammal Protection Act. Polar bears have remained important as a source of meat for Iñupiaq villagers, and the hides are still used for clothing and traditional crafts. But polar bear hunting seems less intense today, and villagers might simply observe animals that approach their communities or drive them off if they forage too boldly near towns.

Far to the east, polar bears that summer along the shores of Hudson Bay have spawned a wildlife-watching industry for the town of Churchill, Manitoba. Nothing of the sort exists in Alaska, but occasionally there are remarkable opportunities here to watch, study, and photograph these animals...as I had discovered for myself along the coast of the Arctic National Wildlife Refuge.

WATER WALKERS

Categorizing polar bears as terrestrial animals is a bit of a stretch, since they depend on the ocean almost as completely as whales or sea lions do. Yet neither are they unambiguously marine mammals, because they spend most their time on solid footing. Perhaps more than any other animal, polar bears are purely creatures of the ice—a remarkable, ephemeral terrain that comes as a gift of cold.

The Arctic ice pack can be appropriately described as a sprawling, frozen continent. But unlike stable continents of bedrock and dirt, the ice terrain perpetually moves with the forces of wind, with the tide, and with the great gyres of polar current; it cleaves into thick slabs that ride over and under each other, piles into enormous mounds and ridges, fractures into networks of cracks and wide leads of open water. When the ice is still and quiet, it seems as solid as the earth itself. But at other times you can watch a vast icescape, stretching off to the far horizon, gliding swiftly by. Remarkably, the ice pack in motion can be completely, bewilderingly silent. But when a drifting floe collides with an expanse of solidly grounded ice, it sounds like the entire planet is groaning. Iñupiaq elders warn that a person who values his life will never go anywhere near colliding ice.

This is one of the most physically complex, tempestuously unpredictable, intellectually challenging environments on earth. And no animal has mastered it like the polar bear.

Everything about these creatures suits them for life on the Arctic ice. Perhaps most obviously, their creamy white fur offers camouflage when they stalk seals, and it helps to conceal them from their only predator—humans. Iñupiaq hunters point out that the bear's fur actually looks yellowish against the purer white of snow. The long, glossy outer hairs easily shed water, while the dense, wooly underfur gives warmth. Equally important, healthy polar bears carry a thick layer of insulating fat. All this, combined with their internal metabolic furnace, sustains a body temperature similar to our own—but under conditions that defy imagination.

On the Beaufort Sea coast, I once saw bears snoozing all day like sunbathers on a white sand beach, oblivious to the subzero temperatures and storm-blown snow sifting over them. Even more impressive, one blizzardy afternoon two bears began stomping on the lagoon ice until they broke a hole, which they enlarged into a pool about 20 yards long. Then they spent several hours playing in the water like puppies—diving, thrashing, wrestling, standing on the fragile edge until the ice caved under them, shaking off great spirals of water, and rolling around on the saturated salty snow.

The polar bear's shape has evolved for a life in and around water. Its body is long and sleek compared to that of a grizzly (*Ursus arctos*, also known as the brown bear), its neck is also conspicuously elongated, and its skull is streamlined. Those broad forepaws are adapted for paddling, while the hind legs trail in the water as rudders. Alaska's whale-bone scavengers have obviously swum long distances to reach land, and there are many reports of ships encountering polar bears paddling beyond the sight of either ice or shore.

RIGHT *The polar bear is mild mannered compared to the sometimes fiercely aggressive grizzly bear, such as this subadult feasting at a whale carcass (autumn, Arctic National Wildlife Refuge).*

URSUS MARITIMUS

Polar bears inhabit an enormous span of the earth's northward circumference, with their greatest numbers near the Arctic coastlines of Alaska, Canada, Greenland, Norway, and Russia. They also roam far out onto the ice pack and have been tracked within 150 miles of the North Pole. But despite their vast range, polar bears are thinly dispersed—biologists estimate there are only about 25,000 in the world today. At least half are in Canadian territory, and 3,000 to 4,000 inhabit the ice-covered waters near Alaska. By comparison, in the state of Alaska alone there are an estimated 30,000 grizzlies and 100,000 black bears.

From a human perspective, the Arctic ice might seem uniform and unbounded, but polar bears separate themselves into more than a dozen distinct populations. One such group inhabits the Chukchi Sea, from northwestern Alaska across to Siberia; another lives on the Beaufort Sea, from Alaska's North Slope into adjacent Canada. Tagged bears have covered tremendous distances within their territories—from 1,000 to 4,000 miles every year. An exceptional wanderer marked at Prudhoe Bay, Alaska, turned up more than 3,000 miles away in northern Greenland. There's still much to be learned about the home ranges of individual polar bears. Some animals stay within an area of several hundred square miles, but studies show that others have home ranges encompassing nearly 100,000 square miles—an area almost the size of Colorado.

For countless generations, Iñupiaq hunters have closely studied polar bears and have passed along their accumulated knowledge. According to the elders, track patterns show that many bears move southward at the beginning of winter, and there is another move-

ment toward the north as spring approaches. Research biologists agree. When the pack ice shrinks northward during the summer months, most Alaskan polar bears stay well off the Arctic coast, favoring the southern margins of the drifting floes.

Polar bears took to the ice 200,000 to 250,000 years ago, when they diverged from a common ancestor with the modern brown bears. Evolutionary studies indicate that polar bears—*Ursus maritimus*—are the youngest of the world's eight bear species. In fact, their emergence is so recent that polar bears and grizzlies have mated and produced offspring in zoos; and a wild polar bear–grizzly hybrid was killed in 2006 by a hunter in the Northwest Territories of Canada.

Like their brown bear cousins, polar bears favor a solitary life—except for mothers with cubs and couples during brief mating liaisons. Congregations around ephemeral food sources like the whale bones can be grumpy affairs, accompanied by hissing, snorting, angry jaw popping, spectacular roaring matches, and occasional brawls. I even saw a mother bear growl at her own cub, pushing it away when the little one snatched a bit of food she had claimed.

On the other hand, the polar bear is mild mannered compared to the sometimes fiercely aggressive grizzly. When grizzlies show up at beach carrion, for example, polar bears usually move off during the day and feed only at night, rather than deal with the hot-tempered interlopers. This is true even though grizzlies living on the North Slope of Alaska are generally much smaller than polar bears. Once cold weather forces the grizzlies to leave for their inland hibernation dens, polar bears are more likely to visit the carrion both day and night.

Nevertheless, polar bears are truly formidable creatures. Watching them rip at the whale bones and argue with each other that day, I marveled at their mass and strength, and I needed no reminder that polar bears share a distinction as the world's largest nonaquatic carnivore—equaled only by the coastal Alaskan brown bear. Adult female polar bears weigh 400 to 700 pounds; the males average 600 to 1,200 pounds, and occasional giants approach 1,700 pounds. Standing on their hind legs, they measure 8 to 10 feet tall.

The power exhibited in their legs, shoulders, and conspicuous array of claws is awesome. Their claws are used for digging, tearing, hunting, and traction—as I saw when the swimming bears scrambled

CLOCKWISE FROM TOP LEFT
Iñupiaq hunter Dale Brower, wearing a parka with a polar-bear ruff, cleans a polar bear skin by dragging it across the ice (spring, Chukchi Sea). The Iñupiat still use the hides for clothing and traditional crafts / The shape of this bear's body, its short neck, and its odd face—when compared to other polar bears in this book—lead one to believe this may be a grizzly bear hybrid (autumn, coastal plain, Arctic National Wildlife Refuge). / Once whale meat from a carcass is gone, polar bears sneak around Kaktovik at night until chased away or all the scraps are gone, then head out onto the ice (autumn, Arctic National Wildlife Refuge). / Polar bears often fight over food at whalebone piles; hissing, snorting, jaw popping, roaring, and brawling are common (coastal plain, Arctic National Wildlife Refuge).

up onto the slick, wet ice around their pond. The soles of a polar bear's feet are partly covered with fur, not just for warmth but also for added traction and for quiet stalking on crisp, frosty snow. In fact, the polar bear's feet may have first inspired Iñupiaq hunters to fasten soft fur onto the bottom of their boots, so they could move silently when they hunt seals at breathing holes.

THE HUNTERS

While the grizzly's diet is heavy on plant foods, polar bears are almost completely carnivorous. Their entire body is a predatory masterwork, combining great size and prodigious strength with a phenomenal sense of smell, acute eyesight, excellent hearing, long canine teeth to grab and kill prey, and powerful molars for shearing and chewing meat. But the polar bear's most remarkable tool, as is true for the humans who share this icy world, is its mind. This is an extraordinarily shrewd and ingenious predator.

Polar bears specialize in hunting seals, but they also occasionally manage to kill walruses, especially pups that they catch away from their formidably defensive mothers. It's a risky proposition, as attested to by Iñupiaq hunters' stories of walruses skewering bears with their tusks. Iñupiaq hunters have occasionally seen a determined polar bear succeed in killing a beluga whale when it rolls up to breathe after becoming trapped at a small opening in the ice. Polar bears have also been observed swimming underwater to snatch unsuspecting seabirds from below. On land, they sometimes catch caribou or musk ox, chase down small prey like ground squirrels and lemmings, pilfer bird eggs, and forage on plants and berries.

The polar bear's most important prey, by far, is the ringed seal—or *natchiq*—an abundant Arctic species that reaches about 150 pounds. Alaskan polar bears also hunt the much larger bearded seal—or *ugruk*—measuring up to 8 feet and 750 pounds. Both ringed and bearded seals spend their entire lives on, around, and under sea ice.

Iñupiaq elders tell fascinating stories of the polar bear's hunting strategies. They say, for example, that a bear will sometimes lie perfectly still at the edge of an open lead or pond—hour after hour—and if a seal rises nearby to breathe, the bear slips into the water, swims under the surface, and grabs its prey from below. Sometimes the bear makes a hole through the thin ice, well back from the edge, where it has a better chance of sliding into the water without alarming its prey.

During the winter, ringed and bearded seals maintain breathing holes—narrow, vertical tunnels through ice that may be 10 feet or more thick—which are often their only source of air. These holes—called *allu* in the Iñupiaq language—are usually marked by a small *iglu*-shaped ice dome with an opening the size of a quarter on top. Learning to prey on seals—which live beneath unbroken winter ice and breathe at these tiny holes—may be the foundation of polar bear evolution and survival.

Using its almost preternatural sense of smell, a polar bear can detect breathing holes up to a mile away, even when they are deeply covered by snow. A Wainwright hunter described following a polar bear's tracks along a great, flat expanse where the animal had located one breathing hole after another, all in thick ice with a light cover of snow. At each hole, the man could read a story written in tracks and diggings. Every time it found an *allu*, the bear had excavated a little trench around the base of the dome to make the ice thinner. I was fascinated to hear his story, because Iñupiaq elders had often told me that polar bears hunt this way.

And then the bear had waited—motionless and silent—always staying downwind from the hole so the seal would not catch a warning scent. If a seal rises in its *allu* to breathe, the man told me, the bear smashes the ice dome with its paw and simultaneously kills the seal, then grabs it with its jaws and pulls it out through the hole. But in this case, despite the bear's patience and perseverance, it had not caught a seal. And after tracking the bear for many miles, the hunter realized he would never overtake it, so he headed back home.

In the spring, both ringed and bearded seals crawl out on the ice to bask and sleep in the endless sunshine. As the old Iñupiaq hunter had first described to me those many years ago, polar bears hunt

Male polar bears average twice the weight of females, and their build is more muscular. Radio-collar studies track only females, because collars won't stay on males, whose necks are larger than their heads.

ABOVE *Unlike grizzlies, which are solitary and unsocial by nature, polar bears often sniff one another when first meeting; note their long necks and streamlined skulls (autumn, coastal plain, Arctic National Wildlife Refuge).*

RIGHT *Polar bears engaging in some sort of dominance, mating, or play behavior*

these animals by making a long, slow stalk, then suddenly dashing to grab the seal or kill it with a powerful swat. Iñupiaq men who have watched these stalks say the bear often slides across the ice, pushing with its hind legs and using its "forearms" like sled runners, so the front part of its body moves very little and acts like a white screen. Iñupiaq elders say that during these hunts, a bear will sometimes use its tongue or paws to cover its conspicuous black nose. Near the whale bones, decades after I first heard about it from my Iñupiaq mentors, I finally saw polar bears sledding this way on their forearms, but for another reason: instead of hunting seals, they were sliding across very thin ice that would probably have broken if they had not spread out their weight and slipped over it quickly.

Also in the springtime, pregnant ringed seals come up through their breathing holes and hollow out caves under piled ice or snow-drifts. In these hidden caverns, they give birth and raise their pups, but not without danger. A polar bear will roam the ice searching for a telltale scent that seeps up through the drift. Then it stealthily approaches the den, rears up on its hind legs, and smashes through the roof, sometimes quickly enough to snatch the mother or her pup before they can escape into the hole. Biologists report that during this season, denning seals are a major source of food for polar bears.

During the spring and summer, polar bears make a kill every four to five days when seals are relatively easy to hunt. Researchers and village hunters agree that the bears often eat only the seal's skin and calorie-rich blubber. Well-fed bears are likely to leave the remaining carcass for scavengers like the dainty white Arctic foxes that often shadow a polar bear's wanderings. Of course, a truly hungry bear eats the entire seal, leaving the foxes nothing more than a bloodstain on the snow.

GENERATIONS

If a polar bear goes beyond a week or so without food, its metabolism automatically slows down to burn less energy. This hedge against weight loss and starvation is another adaptation to the uncertainties

RIGHT *Fresh tracks across the Arctic ice pack—a sprawling, frozen continent perpetually moving with the forces of wind, tides, and polar currents*

of life on the Arctic ice. By contrast, grizzlies and black bears are more vulnerable to food shortages because their metabolism slows only during the protracted dormancy of their midwinter hibernation.

Polar bears divide their time between traveling around, resting among the drifts and ridges, and hunting their prey. From late March into May, the males roam widely, following the tracks and alluring scents of females. If a male encounters a female in estrus—or mating readiness—the two keep romantic company for a few days, after which the male wanders off to search for other willing consorts.

The presence of seals allows polar bears to stay active all winter despite the protracted darkness, deep cold, and apparent emptiness of the unbroken ice. The pregnant female is an important exception. Sometime between late November and mid-December in Arctic Alaska, she digs a snow cave either on the pack ice fairly close to shore or on land not far from the sea. The den usually tunnels into a large drift (which often gets deeper as the winter progresses), with an oval chamber at the end. In some cases, at least, the entrance tunnel starts low on the drift and slopes upward, which helps to trap warmth from the bear's breath and body. It may seem paradoxical, but snow is an excellent insulator, so the temperature inside a den stays just a few degrees below freezing, despite shuddering blizzards and minus-50-degree nights.

Although polar bears mate in spring, the fertilized eggs live in a kind of suspended animation for many months, and only after the female enters her den will they implant in the uterine wall and begin to develop. After an extremely short pregnancy—probably sometime in late December or early January—one or two (and rarely three) furless cubs are born, each weighing about a pound and a half. In a sense, the den is like a kangaroo's pouch, where semi-embryonic young are born and continue their development outside the mother's body.

The cubs grow quickly on their mother's milk, which is almost 50 percent fat, reaching 15 to 25 pounds by March or April, when they leave the den. Young polar bears stay with their mother for the next two years, mastering the skills they will need to hunt and survive in their frozen world. Many young bears don't make it through their first year of independence. They die mainly of starvation, but some

are taken by human hunters and a few are killed by other polar bears.

Females have their first cubs at around age six, followed by new litters about every three years. Male polar bears live to about twenty-five years (rarely into their thirties), while females reach an average maximum age of thirty. So a female has cubs only about five times in her life—a very slow reproductive rate imposed by the stringent demands of the Arctic environment. For this reason, once a polar bear population declines, it is very slow to rebuild.

Not surprisingly, there are words in the Iñupiaq language specific to a polar bear's age, gender, or other circumstances. For example, *nanuayaaq* is a small cub; a second-year cub still traveling with its mother is called *atiqtaq*; an adult female keeping company with her almost fully grown cubs is *atiqtagrualik*; *avinnaaq* is the name for a young bear recently independent from its mother.

INTERWOVEN LIVES

An interplanetary visitor who learned about the remarkable life of the polar bear might logically assume that no other animal could have the genius and toughness to survive on the Arctic ice. But of course, the Iñupiat of Alaska and closely related Canadian Inuit people have thrived in this same environment for many thousands of years. They have carefully studied polar bears, shared the ice with them as fellow predators of seals and other animals, hunted the bears themselves, and have sometimes become the bear's prey.

According to Iñupiaq elders, men were particularly at risk in the old days, when they stayed out on the ice all night tending seal nets, especially in the times before firearms. I heard about a man who was confronted by a bear and faced it down with only his knife, warning the animal, "You'd better leave me alone, or I will cut your handsome face." After a protracted standoff, the man returned safely to his village and the bear headed away onto the pack. Of course, polar bears can become a threat especially when they are pursued or wounded;

CLOCKWISE FROM TOP LEFT
Snacking on a ring-billed gull (fall, coastal plain, Arctic National Wildlife Refuge) / Subadults play-wrestle. / This cub bites its mother, challenging her for her food. / The sow bites back, letting her cub know who's boss.

there are modern stories of angered bears chasing snow machines. But while Iñupiaq hunters clearly respect these animals, they seem almost completely undaunted by them.

Perhaps indigenous people have long understood what researchers are discovering: polar bears tend to be curious and fearless toward humans, far more than actually dangerous. For example, a study on bear-human conflict in Alaska by U.S. Geological Survey biologists Tom Smith and Steven Herrero revealed only seven "incidents" between polar bears and humans over the century between 1900 and 2002, and these resulted in just two confirmed injuries and a single fatality. They concluded that "polar bears have not lived up to the commonly held belief that they—above all other bears—will stalk and hunt down a human." Not surprisingly, the statistics showed that grizzlies are incomparably more dangerous than polar bears.

Like their compatriots in modern science, Iñupiaq people have been far more interested in learning about polar bears than fearing them. Their connections with these animals are ancient, complex, and perhaps deeper than we might first imagine. I began thinking about this when Iñupiaq hunters taught me how to walk on thin ice by gliding steadily along with my legs spread, so that my weight was always moving and distributed as widely as possible. If the ice still threatened to break, they advised, I should splay myself down on all fours and, as a last resort, belly along with outstretched arms and legs. Each time my instructors repeated this crucial lesson, they were almost sure to add: "That's how the polar bear does it."

I sensed that they made this point to confirm the authority and reliability of their advice. Polar bears may have perfected the spread-legged technique for crossing thin ice a hundred thousand years before humans wandered onto the floes. So I was led to wonder: Did ancestral Iñupiaq people learn by watching polar bears? Just how closely intertwined are the lives of these two crafty, sharp-witted, keenly observant Arctic predators?

LEFT *An Iñupiaq elder warned, "Polar bears are left-handed … If a bear charges at you, his left paw is going to be the quickest one, so you should jump to his right side. There's a better chance he'll miss you with that paw" (autumn, coastal plain, Arctic National Wildlife Refuge).*

THE LEFT-HANDED BEAR

Iñupiaq people, like their neighbors across Canada and Greenland, hunt seals that sleep and bask on the ice in almost exactly the same way as the polar bears do. Wearing clothes that match the whiteness of ice and snow, the hunter crawls toward the seal whenever it lays its head down to sleep, and when it snaps awake to check for danger, the hunter keeps perfectly still. In former times, when the stalker came close enough, he sprinted to the seal and struck it with a harpoon. The same method is used today, but hunters need to sneak only within accurate shooting range.

Is it possible that ancient Iñupiaq people learned to hunt sleeping seals by observing polar bears?

Iñupiaq people often told me about their experiences watching polar bears, with all the fascination and discipline of the most expert naturalists. For example, an elder from Barrow, Alaska, told me that he once hid behind an ice ridge through the long twilight hours of a spring night, overlooking a broad ice flat where a polar bear was poised beside a seal's breathing hole. The bear would slowly lift one of its feet from the moist, salty ice and hold it in the air for a while, then very gently bring it down and just as carefully lift another foot. "He kept doing that through the whole night," the old man recalled, "taking turns getting his feet off the ice so they could warm up a little."

This is just one small story among thousands that have been told every year across the Arctic, in camps and villages, century after century, down through the millennia. Observations like these have been endlessly tested, repeated, and refined. Taken together, they explain why people like the Iñupiat have amassed a prodigious knowledge of their world.

This knowledge can be crucially important when a hunter goes looking for bears. I heard a remarkable story from a Wainwright man who had wounded a polar bear that suddenly came pounding across the ice in a full charge. "When a bear comes straight toward you like that, it's really hard to get a good shot," he warned. "You can't hit the neck. You can't hit the shoulder or heart. And your bullet might glance off that bear's skull."

But the man knew exactly what to do. As the bear hurtled toward him, he steadied his aim and waited...until the bear was close enough for an extremely difficult precision shot into the bulging muscles of the animal's hindquarter. He was fully aware that the impact alone could not halt a charging bear, but it would cause a bolt of pain. Precisely as he expected, the bear stopped, turned, and bit the wound—as if by an involuntary reflex—exposing its neck to a final deadly shot.

I marveled at the man's certainty during those intense, interminable seconds. It was one of many times when I saw that an Iñupiaq hunter's survival depends on the unbroken thread of traditional knowledge.

During my year-long apprenticeship with Iñupiaq people, I heard many stories and lessons that were hard to believe at first, but experience later showed that they were true. This is why I listened closely when an elder advised me, "Polar bears are left-handed. It's something you always need to remember. If a bear charges at you, his left paw is going to be the quickest one. So you should jump to his right side. There's a better chance he'll miss you with that paw."

I've never had an opportunity to see left-handedness in a polar bear—and biologists have concluded that polar bears seem to use their right and left paws equally—but I definitely know which way I would jump!

We newcomers to the Arctic are beginning to recognize that the Iñupiaq people's knowledge is much more than an intriguing artifact in the museum of human intellect. It may have profound significance in our efforts to fully document climate change, to understand the impact of warming temperatures on all that lives in the northern world, and to recognize the implications of these changes for human communities far beyond the icy realms of the polar bear.

THE VANISHING CONTINENT

The polar bear and the Iñupiaq people have thrived together for millennia in one of the earth's most extreme environments. Responding to the opportunities and challenges of this environment has given rise to their parallel, intertwined genius. But as the other essays in this book reveal, and as we learn from the growing volumes of scientific research on climate change, polar bears and Iñupiaq people are facing a challenge far more perilous than any other in their history. Climatic warming, in large part fueled by industrial technology, imminently threatens the existence of their shared world.

Struggling to comprehend this possibility, I try to imagine the solid earth beneath our nation rapidly and inexorably dissolving and all that sustains us disappearing with it: forests and meadows, croplands and pastures, towns and cities.

Some potential responses to climate change are global and long-term; others are more localized and immediate, perhaps easier to grasp. For example, as I hunkered against the cold watching the mother bear that October day, I realized that her twin cubs may have been born somewhere nearby during the previous winter. In fact, the surrounding coast of the Arctic National Wildlife Refuge has the highest historical density of polar bear birthing dens in Alaska. Recent trends show increasing numbers of dens on land and along the coast west of the refuge. The United States is the only Arctic nation that does not have a sanctuary designated specifically for these bears, but the Arctic Refuge serves this role. It is also the only protected public wildland in America where polar bears are known to regularly den and give birth.

According to both scientists and Iñupiaq elders, female polar bears may abandon their den if they are disturbed, and any cubs left behind will not survive. This lends added importance to the Arctic Refuge and makes it imperative that the area remain isolated from human activity during the winter months. For this reason, polar bears have become a significant concern in debates over creating a major petrochemical complex within the refuge.

LOOKING IN THE BEAR'S EYES

A strengthening gale filled the air with whirling snow, and the visible world shrank to a dim, pallid circle a few hundred yards across. The mother bear seemed completely, comfortably at home, as if the blizzard made her feel more secure. If any other bears were near, they were hidden by the whiteout. The bear lifted her nose, probing the wind for scents; she made her way to the sheltered lee of the whale bones and lay down on the drift like a dog curling up in a cozy living room. Moments later the two cubs snuggled against her, resting their heads on her thick belly fur. Gusts buffeted through the bones, and powder snow quickly accumulated on her back.

The cubs soon fell asleep, but their mother only napped, raising her head at intervals to test the wind and glance away toward the ice. I sat quietly, feeling both safe and vulnerable in the presence of these bears, while the chill crept into my heavy parka and snow pants. My thoughts wandered back forty years, to my experiences as a young apprentice in Wainwright. I had come across polar bear tracks dozens of times out on the pack ice—but never once did I catch sight of their makers. Somehow this made everything about the present moment seem even more precious, more exquisite...more impossible.

Finally the mother bear relaxed and put her chin on her paws, and for several minutes she held me in a protracted, unwavering gaze.

I looked toward her and away, careful to avoid what might seem like an aggressive stare. And I wondered: What does this polar bear know that I could never fathom—about traveling on the ice, living through storms, meeting others of her kind, nursing cubs in a snow cave, stalking walruses on the summer floes, waiting for seals at their breathing holes? What understanding of the Arctic world is woven through the pathways of her mind? What could I learn in a lifetime of tracking polar bears across the ice, as generations of Iñupiaq hunters have done? And what secrets could she reveal to us about this land now in peril?

The mother bear gently nuzzled her cubs, rested her head on the snow, and shut her eyes. Unfastened from her gaze, I felt a sudden ache of loss, imagining how the earth would be diminished if the great ice pack should disappear and with it the polar bear, the ringed seal, the walrus, the bearded seal, and innumerable other creatures of this frozen world. Along with them, the traditions and knowledge of Iñupiaq people and their kin—born over countless millennia through an intimate relationship with the ice and its living community—would also become extinct.

A darkening rush of clouds brought on the early Arctic dusk. It was time to leave.

During my last minutes there, I allowed myself an inward, prayerful hope—that polar bears and Iñupiaq people might always thrive here at the northern fringe of life on earth. And I imagined a village beside a vast, moving, jumbled continent of ice, where a child sang out the ancient names for polar bear: *Nanuayaaq. Atiqtaq. Atiqtagrualik. Avinnaaq. Nanuq.*

The cubs wrapped themselves tightly against the comforting warmth of their mother's belly. And she slept.

Richard Nelson is a writer, activist, cultural anthropologist, and subsistence hunter who lives in Southeast Alaska. His books include Patriotism and the American Land, Make Prayers to the Raven *(which became an award-winning PBS television series),* Hunters of the Northern Forest, Shadow of the Hunter, *and* Hunters of the Northern Ice. *Nelson's awards include the John Burroughs Medal for nature writing for* The Island Within, *the Sigurd Olson Nature Writing Award for* Heart and Blood: Living with Deer in America, *a National Endowment for the Arts Fellowship, and a Lannan Literary Award for nonfiction. He hosts his own radio show and speaks publicly on his work and on issues of conservation. In the words of author Jim Harrison, the magic of Nelson's writing is that it speaks to "hunters and anti-hunters, environmentalists and politicians, and anyone who cares about what's left of the natural world in America."*

Terrestrial Coastal Environment

Wherever they live, animals depend on plants or other animals for food. The images on these pages show parts of the tundra food web in the Arctic.

TOP ROW, LEFT TO RIGHT *Arctic mushrooms amid fall foliage; plant-eating animals include lemmings, ptarmigans, caribou, and hares. / Collared lemmings and other small rodents are common prey for foxes. / Arctic ground squirrel, preyed on by foxes and grizzlies / Snowshoe hares are prey for foxes. / Rock ptarmigan in winter plumage, also prey for foxes / White-fronted goose, a migrating bird that nests on Arctic tundra*

BOTTOM ROW, RIGHT TO LEFT *Caribou feed on plants; predators include grizzlies and wolves. / Musk oxen are preyed upon by grizzlies and wolves. / Short-eared owls feed on small rodents and carrion. / Red fox kits outside their den; they eat rodents, squirrels, hares, and birds. / Wolverines feed on carrion and small mammals, in addition to bird eggs, berries, and insects. / Grizzlies are at the top of the food chain: they eat everything.*

Culpability crosses socioeconomic, cultural, and geographic lines. Can we summon the collective will to adapt, as in the past, and reinvent ourselves?

Nick Jans

Living with Oil: The Real Price

ALASKA AIRLINES FLIGHT 146 IS FULL—Iñupiaq Eskimos, other North Slope residents, and a few tasseled-loafer types mixed into the crowd. Most passengers, though, fit a narrow profile: predominately male and Caucasian, clad in canvas jackets, coveralls, and ball caps. Five miles below, the jumbled crags of the Alaska Range roll past, glowing incandescent pink in the fading rays of the low December sun.

We're headed across the Arctic Circle and as far north as Alaska gets, where that same sun hasn't cleared the horizon in three weeks, and won't for several more. Barrow, the northernmost community in the United States, is the destination for some of us. But most people on this plane are long-distance commuters bound for the Oil Patch, the sprawling network of producing fields and exploratory activity radiating outward from Prudhoe Bay, itself the largest oil field in North America. The development stretches across the west-central edge of Alaska's North Slope, and ever farther west into the National Petroleum Reserve–Alaska (NPRA)—a humming, industrial organism whose steel veins pulse with warm crude. Pumped from miles-deep strata, gathered through a geometric maze of feeder lines, strained through pump and flow stations, the oil streams southward, 1,100 miles down the Trans-Alaska Pipeline to the port of Valdez in south-central Alaska. There it's loaded onto tankers bound for West Coast or Asian refineries, and on to the world's ever-thirsty gas pumps.

"I'm here for one reason, dude, and one reason only," nodded a twentysomething laborer from Utah I met at the airport check-in counter. "The money. I almost got enough saved to buy me a new truck." He shook his head, as if dazed by his good fortune. Polar bears? Well, he grinned, there was that big stuffed one in the glass case at the end of the concourse. Like most North Slope oil workers

(and most Alaskans, for that matter), he'd never seen a live one in the wild and wasn't likely to.

From up in the plane, the light fades to purple tones. On my left sits an affable guy with a desperado mustache and a logo-emblazoned jacket. He's the chief of an exploration crew that's been working in Wyoming and is moving north for the season. The giant mobile rig he's in charge of has the capacity to drill as deep as 20,000 feet—from the summit of Mount McKinley (which we've just passed) down to sea level. The crew will spend the next four months drilling where the geologists point, probing for new pockets of oil. The Arctic winter, with its brutal conditions, is high season for exploration—a window that's narrowed by four to eight weeks over the past three decades, as later freeze-ups and earlier thaws have cut down the time when protective, leveling ice roads can be laid, transforming unstable wet tundra into pathways for moving heavy equipment. Meanwhile, exploration on the North Slope, like development of existing fields, is booming—expanding at a rate unequaled even in the heady days of the '70s and early '80s."That's why we're here," says the crew boss. "This is what's happening."

The 1,000 square miles encompassed by Prudhoe and the twenty-odd neighboring oil fields abut the polar bears' world and are poised to expand into it—both into onshore denning areas and offshore into the heart of their pack-ice hunting grounds in the Beaufort and Chukchi seas, where enormous oil lease sales are scheduled. And, as the bears are forced to spend more and more time ashore as a result of that ever-lengthening summer thaw, and as more pregnant females seem forced to den onshore, as a 2007 U.S. Geological Survey study reports, their footprints (actual and metaphorical) and that of oil are bound to increasingly overlap. That said, there's no evidence, scientific or anecdotal, to suggest that North Slope oil infrastructure—the actual pipelines, wells, roads, and

LEFT *The Trans-Alaska pipeline crosses tundra and mountains from the Beaufort Sea at Prudhoe Bay to Valdez on Prince William Sound (autumn, north of the Brooks Range).*

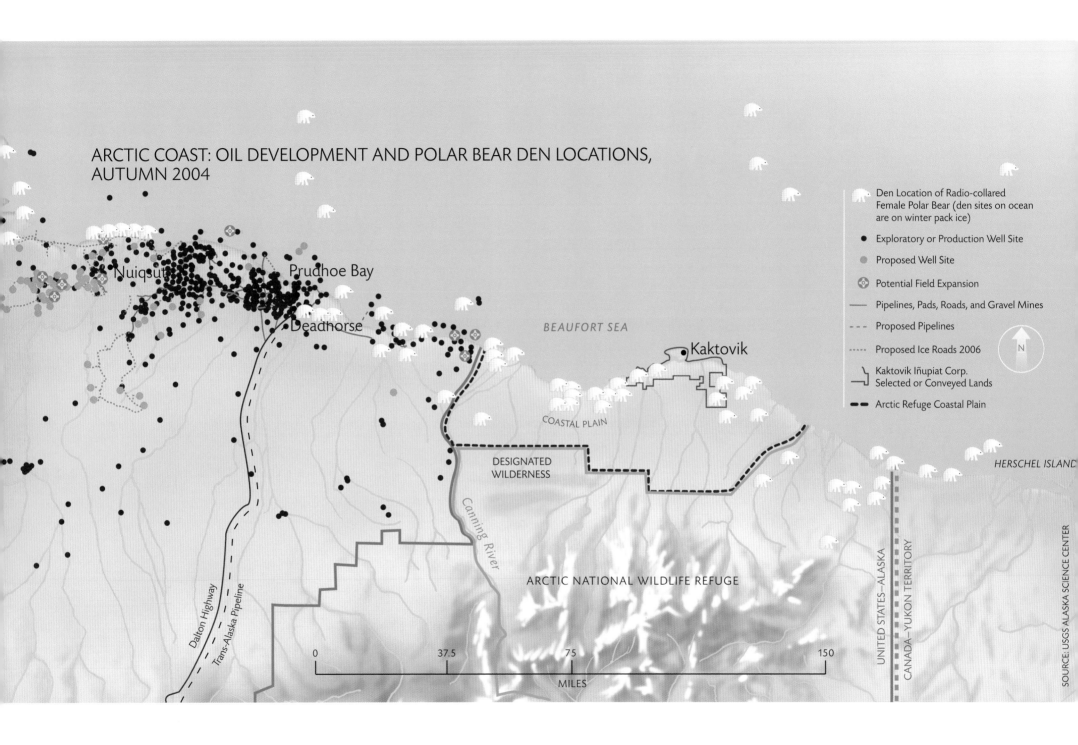

ARCTIC COAST: OIL DEVELOPMENT AND POLAR BEAR DEN LOCATIONS, AUTUMN 2004

Nuiqsut

Prudhoe Bay

Deadhorse

BEAUFORT SEA

Kaktovik

COASTAL PLAIN

DESIGNATED WILDERNESS

Canning River

ARCTIC NATIONAL WILDLIFE REFUGE

HERSCHEL ISLAND

Dalton Highway

Trans-Alaska Pipeline

UNITED STATES–ALASKA

CANADA–YUKON TERRITORY

Den Location of Radio-collared Female Polar Bear (den sites on ocean are on winter pack ice)

● Exploratory or Production Well Site

● Proposed Well Site

⊕ Potential Field Expansion

— Pipelines, Pads, Roads, and Gravel Mines

--- Proposed Pipelines

···· Proposed Ice Roads 2006

Kaktovik Iñupiat Corp. Selected or Conveyed Lands

▬▬ Arctic Refuge Coastal Plain

N

0   37.5   75   150

MILES

SOURCE: USGS ALASKA SCIENCE CENTER

so on—is so far directly affecting polar bear numbers or their overall chances for survival.

Neither are current oil-field emissions a serious factor. "Exploration and drilling don't in themselves cause global warming," says Daren Beaudo, director of press relations for BP Alaska, one of the "big three" megacorporate players in North Slope oil (ExxonMobile and ConocoPhillips round out the trio, and a number of smaller companies hold varying stakes). Of course, Beaudo is right. While exploration activities and production facilities themselves do produce clouds of greenhouse gases, the total amount of Alaska's oil-field emissions is, at worst, equal to that of a moderate-sized U.S. city. Oil-field air pollution is far more a local than a global issue.

The true impact of oil, whether from wells in Alaska, Saudi Arabia, or Venezuela, occurs thousands of miles away from the fields themselves and in banal, incremental acts—turning the ignition key on the family car, bumping up a thermostat, flying cross-country on a jet, flicking a light switch—made billions of times, by billions of people, day after week after year. No question that some folks burn more than others; affluence and consumption and exhaust gases seem inextricably twined. The citizens of the United States and other "first-world" countries are first as well in per capita production of greenhouse-gas emissions. Despite our best intentions, those of us who can afford a caring, global perspective are paradoxically the gas-guzzling super-SUVs of our species. We don't seem able to help ourselves, even though effective measures to reduce our individual oil intake and consequent exhaust of greenhouse gases lie within our grasp. Shaking our fist at Big Oil and at governmental inaction while we write a check to our favorite conservation organization is far more gratifying than peering into a mirror or imagining the crystals of ice that melt under a bear's paws each time we press the gas pedal and merge into endless lanes of people doing the same thing.

Culpability by participation—conscious or otherwise—crosses socioeconomic, cultural, and geographic borders. To a greater or lesser degree, most of us *Homo sapiens* are cogs in the vast economic engine fueled by hydrocarbon consumption—one that threatens the survival of not only the bears but quite possibly ourselves as well. In the words of cartoonist Walt Kelly, we have met the enemy and he is

us. The questions remain: What are we going to do with that realization? Can we summon the collective will to adapt, as we have before, and reinvent ourselves?

The realities of living with oil are literal and immediate for the Alaska North Slope Iñupiat—a word that means literally, the People. Like the white bears, both their past and their future remain tied to the land that shaped them. What separates the two, one might argue, is that human capacity for adaptation. I sit in the spacious, modern office of Edward Itta, mayor of the North Slope Borough. "I grew up in the days of dog teams and burning whale blubber in stoves to warm our houses," he says. "No running water, no electricity." His family moved with the seasons as they hunted and gathered. Today, he sits behind an executive's desk, an avuncular, well-spoken man in his early sixties. The life-size outline of a bowhead whale's pectoral flipper covers one wall and, arranged within it, the actual bones, startlingly like an enormous human forearm and hand—not a trophy, but a tribute. Itta commands a local whaling crew, one of several dozen that spend weeks out on the ice each spring through fall. The hunt, and the sharing and celebration that follow the taking of a whale, remain intensely communal activities, as they have for centuries. "The whale," he explains, "is the centerpiece of our culture. It holds the coastal Iñupiat together. If we lose the great whale and the environment that sustains it, we lose ourselves.

"I was antidevelopment as a young man," he tells me. "A rebel. I had an uncle that was dead set against any inference that we did not own all the land on which we'd always lived. He understood all of the consequences." (Itta is referring to the Alaska Native Claims Settlement Act of 1971, ANCSA, which organized Alaska's Native groups into corporations and paid $1 billion plus 44 million acres—10 percent of the state—as compensation for any and all claims.) He continues, "He told me after ANCSA, 'We have sold out. Now we're not owners of our own destiny.'"

In a rambling narrative tinged with self-deprecating humor, Itta recounts his personal journey—serving in Vietnam, then living in the Lower 48, returning to Barrow in the early '70s. He ended up laboring as a roustabout on drill rig number 29, which turned out to be the confirmation well for Discovery, Prudhoe's first big oil strike.

"Little did I know what was to come. Now I'm sitting here, enjoying the tax revenues for our borough, along with the rest of our people." He flashes a wry smile.

I remind myself that in traditional Iñupiaq storytelling, the true message often lies between the words. Iñupiaq logic, too, often embraces paradox or seemingly contradictory information—a trait that seems admirably suited to expressing the emotions and realities engendered by oil development. Oil is bad; oil is good: these two value statements aren't necessarily the polar opposites Western minds might perceive.

"I support oil development onshore," Itta continues. "It built our infrastructure—schools, public works, local government, law enforcement, and so on—and we depend on continuing revenues to maintain it. But there has to be a reasoned, careful approach. These days, everybody's in such a rush—too much, too soon, too fast, without developing adequate environmental baseline data."

Itta describes the massive cultural changes he's witnessed. "In the space of one generation, money became king up here. It's not all bad, but it's been a major factor in losing some of our cultural values. Alcohol, drugs, materialism...we spend all this time and money studying the environment, but what about the human cost?"

The mayor harbors a pragmatic awareness of the forces that industry and government—both state and federal—have brought to bear on the North Slope. "We've become pretty politically astute these days," he says. "The oil companies are going to follow the rules and go where they're allowed to. At the same time, I recognize that the oil companies can exercise powerful lobbying to make those rules...I think the federal government is a long way from enlightened when it comes to the important things." He evokes the language from broken treaties of the past: "'As long as the rivers flow and the grass is green'...yeah, right." He flashes a sardonic smile.

Itta's laid-back demeanor fades at the mention of offshore lease sales. He acknowledges that the North Slope Borough exercises no jurisdiction over these federally owned and administered areas—and stands to make no profit if oil strikes are made, while facing a potential environmental catastrophe in their traditional hunting grounds. "As for drilling out in that moving ice, I'm adamantly opposed. I say

not only no, but hell no. Too much is at stake. The oil companies have not demonstrated the least ability to conduct a cleanup in Arctic ice, even under perfect conditions. One big spill, and we lose everything, and no amount of money can bring it back. We were here before oil, and we'll have to live here when it's gone." He gestures toward a painting on the wall, which depicts an Eskimo hunter with his head down, spear across his lap, stranded on a perilously small, drifting chunk of ice. "I call that one 'bad planning.'"

AS I WALK THE BRIGHTLY LIT STREETS of Barrow, a city transformed by the economics of oil, there's not a polar bear in sight. The community, population roughly 4,500, consists of modern frame structures laid out in a tidy but wide-flung, wind-pummeled, utterly treeless grid. Thirty years ago everyone walked; now they drive or call a cab. Propane from a local wellhead supplies cheap heat and electrical power, while gasoline, currently around $4.50 a gallon, is barged from Seattle. In the shadow of one of the world's great oil fields, the irony is inescapable—but economics dictate reality: a market this small and remote couldn't support a local refinery. Nonetheless, modern Iñupiat are every bit as dependent on oil as other Americans are—and, given the length of supply lines, even more vulnerable than Lower 48 residents to a disruption in gas supplies. In a world where dog teams, snowshoes, and kayaks have given way to snowmobiles and outboard motors, the People have one foot planted in a fading past, another in the onrushing present.

At noon, the southern sky is suffused with the pale glow of almost-sunrise already fading into a night twenty hours long. A sharp, insistent east wind sifts a rolling haze of snow along the ground, but for mid-December the temperature is positively balmy: plus 19 degrees Fahrenheit. A generation ago 20, even 30, below zero would

CLOCKWISE FROM TOP LEFT
Polar bears near an airfield (Kaktovik, Arctic National Wildlife Refuge) / Military fuel drums are a by-product of the cold war (autumn, Kaktovik, Arctic National Wildlife Refuge). / A grizzly bear sow and her cubs on the shore near Prudhoe Bay; in a warming Arctic, grizzlies may compete more with polar bears for habitat. / As permafrost melts and rising sea levels eat away at the shoreline, erosion uncovers old buried trash, such as this military site from post-WWII's distant early warning (DEW) line (Barter Island, Arctic National Wildlife Refuge).

ABOVE *At times here, the wind sounds as though the skin of the earth is being peeled off (coastal plain, Arctic National Wildlife Refuge).*

have been the norm. The last few days amount to more than some freakish warm spell; this year, the sea ice has yet to become shorefast. Not so many years ago, solid freeze-up occurred by the end of October, without fail. Now it's six, even ten weeks later, and the ice proves thinner and less stable. The elders shake their heads, bemused as if palm trees had sprouted on the shores of the Beaufort Sea. They're beyond debating climate change. It's staring them right in the face.

North Slope Borough biologist Craig George, a passionate advocate for Iñupiaq culture as well as the Arctic ecosystems he studies, comments, "The retreat of the sea ice in just the thirty years I've lived here is astonishing. In years past, you could tell when the sea ice set up in fall by the arrival of polar bears in the village or near Point Barrow...now it is not uncommon to see them along the barrier islands in summer." This ongoing alteration of offshore ice doesn't seem to be negatively affecting all species equally. While polar bears and seals may be threatened, hunters and biologists agree that bowhead whale numbers are steadily increasing and that more open water probably favors the whales—at least for the time being. And onshore, caribou, fish, and migrating waterfowl remain abundant, though the vectors governing species and ecosystems are only partially understood. The patterns of Arctic change, as well as shifting human perspectives, defy sound-bite summation.

While North Slope residents take this warming as fact, they remain divided regarding the ever-expanding presence of oil. Says Richard Glenn of the Arctic Slope Regional Corporation (ASRC), "We're like people everywhere: a spectrum of views from hard left to hard right." As vice president in charge of lands for ASRC, his job is to help coordinate the course of oil development on behalf of the region's 9,000-plus Iñupiaq shareholders. ASRC, as a for-profit Native corporation, owns roughly 5 million acres on the Arctic Slope, carved on the map into a grid of rectangular, coded blocks. Naturally, Glenn's stance is prodevelopment.

"The question is," Glenn says, "is the land big enough and are we big enough to tolerate industry? What do we take and what do we

RIGHT *Polar bears often take advantage of their height, standing on their hind feet to survey the landscape (coastal plain, Arctic National Wildlife Refuge).*

leave? As a hunter and a co-captain of a whaling crew, I feel appropriately conflicted." Glenn, himself half-Iñupiaq and half-Caucasian, with a master's degree in geology and an abiding love for his hunter-gatherer tradition, seems to embody the melding of two worlds. "Sometimes I look in the mirror," he grins, "and ask, 'who am I?'" Like Itta, he seems to possess a nuanced, almost poetic awareness of the cultural and economic contradictions he and his people face—issues not so different from those confronting the rest of the world.

Discussing future oil development on the North Slope, Glenn exudes a confidence verging on bravado. "Some say we're in bed with the devil. But I feel we can take the best of modern and traditional worlds and combine them without surrendering anything. Look at the beautiful parts of our culture—never taking more than you need, for example. This jibes with the notion of sustainable development." I can't help wondering where the tipping points lie between natural optimism, traditional perspective, and corporate duty, and I'm sure Glenn often ponders the same thing.

At times, an outsider might be discomfited by the local vision of stewardship. Glenn, like Mayor Itta and many North Slope Iñupiat, believes that the centerpiece of the Alaska environmental movement, the coastal plain of the Arctic National Wildlife Refuge (ANWR), can be developed with minimal impact—and should be, if it indeed holds a significant reserve of oil. The 1002 Area, of greatest interest to geologists, lies within boundaries where the North Slope Iñupiat would gain royalties from a strike. Both men downplay the area's importance as a vital calving ground and summer habitat for the Porcupine caribou herd (as well as an onshore denning area for female polar bears), claiming that too much ado has been made over too little. Glenn and Itta consider the far-less-publicized Teshekpuk Lake area—a vast coastal wetland east of Barrow, important as a calving ground to the Central Artic caribou herd and a nesting area for

CLOCKWISE FROM TOP LEFT
Playing with an old, discarded tire (autumn, coastal plain, Arctic National Wildlife Refuge) / Naptime on a pressure ridge (summer, Chukchi Sea) / On alert (autumn, coastal plain, Arctic National Wildlife Refuge) / Peeking through a snowdrift (autumn, coastal plain, Arctic National Wildlife Refuge)

hundreds of thousands of waterfowl, now threatened by oil-lease sales—to be of far greater importance. Says Itta, "With ANWR, we're paying for the sins of the Lower 48."

The Iñupiat perspective on the refuge's coastal plain stands in sharp contrast to that of the Gwich'in—the Athapaskan Indian people who live to the south, inside the tree line, and depend on the migrating Porcupine caribou herd for their subsistence needs. Luci Beach, director of the Gwich'in Steering Committee, calls drilling in the refuge "a moral choice for the United States." Unlike the Iñupiat, who share directly in oil revenues from leases on their lands, the Gwich'in stand to gain little from such development—a modest trickle-down share of oil profits—and much to lose. The caribou on which they depend calve and spend the summer on ground that the Gwich'in don't own. The Alaska Native Claims Settlement Act dictated boundaries of ownership that ignore wildlife migration patterns and traditional Native use.

Beach separates the Gwich'in concern for the refuge from the larger question: "I believe, like many of my people, that climate change is global, not local, and that oil is the root cause. But we face a more immediate issue. The Porcupine caribou herd has sustained the Gwich'in since time immemorial. It's our duty to protect them, and the refuge's coastal plain, which we call 'the sacred place where all life begins.'" As far as the difference of opinion with the Iñupiat, she says, "We understand their concerns and support [their point of view]. We hope they will do the same for us."

Regarding polar bears, Luci Beach remains understandably silent. The Gwich'in live and hunt hundreds of miles south of the nearest white bear; they stand less chance of ever seeing one in the wild than that young oil-field worker I met at the Anchorage airport. And though bears certainly are part of the Iñupiaq world, most people in Barrow also seldom speak of them unless prompted. To a pragmatic, subsistence-oriented people, these consummate predators are a respected part of the landscape, but hardly charismatic icons representing some larger issue. When asked which large animals matter most, the coastal Iñupiat speak of their staff of life: bowhead whales first, followed closely by caribou and seals. The Gwich'in rank caribou foremost, then moose. If we outsiders walked in their world, we'd

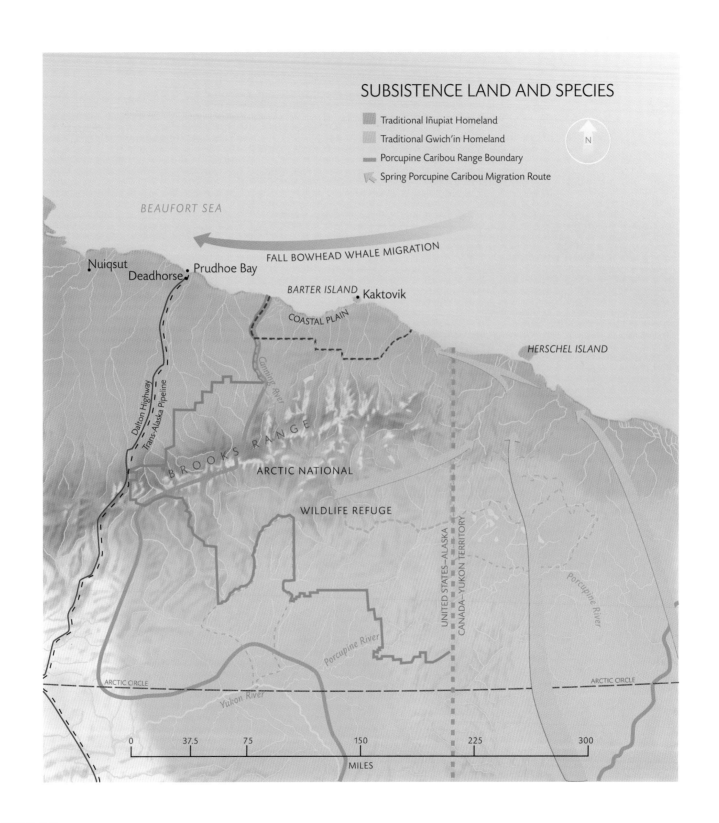

SUBSISTENCE LAND AND SPECIES

- Traditional Iñupiat Homeland
- Traditional Gwich'in Homeland
- Porcupine Caribou Range Boundary
- Spring Porcupine Caribou Migration Route

N

BEAUFORT SEA

FALL BOWHEAD WHALE MIGRATION

Nuiqsut
Deadhorse
Prudhoe Bay
BARTER ISLAND
Kaktovik
COASTAL PLAIN
HERSCHEL ISLAND

Canning River

Dalton Highway
Trans-Alaska Pipeline

BROOKS RANGE

ARCTIC NATIONAL

WILDLIFE REFUGE

UNITED STATES–ALASKA
CANADA–YUKON TERRITORY

Porcupine River

Porcupine River

ARCTIC CIRCLE

ARCTIC CIRCLE

Yukon River

| 0 | 37.5 | 75 | 150 | 225 | 300 |

MILES

Sport hunting for polar bears
ended in the United States with
passage of the Marine Mammal
Protection Act in 1972;
a 1976 treaty extended
the same protection across
the Arctic.

ABOVE *A caribou on summer tundra near a Prudhoe Bay oil development.
The Gwich'in people depend on caribou for their subsistence lifestyle the way
the Iñupiat depend on bowhead whales.*

RIGHT *Moose are also an important food source for the Gwich'in, as seals
are for the Iñupiat (autumn, coastal plain, Arctic National Wildlife Refuge).*

ABOVE *Polar bears prowl newly formed ice, waiting for freeze-up so they can hunt seals (autumn, coastal plain, Arctic National Wildlife Refuge).*

think the same way. What unites us is a steadfast attention to our unique cultural perspectives and economic interests. To the Gwich'in, the caribou are their bank account.

As Richard Glenn intimated, divisive opinions on North Slope oil development exist among the Iñupiat as well. Few of the 480-some residents of Nuiqsut, an hour's flight east of Barrow, share either Glenn's enthusiasm or optimism. Surrounded by ConocoPhillips's rapidly expanding, state-of-the-art Alpine oil field and its satellites, these people find themselves living in the shadow of oil—breathing its exhaust, surrounded by ever-expanding, interconnected islands of steel floating like mirages on the tundra, where just eight years before there were only a handful of exploration crews scattered across a seemingly limitless expanse. Now, armed security guards in late-model pickups patrol field boundaries.

"They let you know you're not welcome," says thirty-year-old Leonard Lampe, president of the village's tribal organization, ex-mayor, and current board member of the Kuukpik Corporation, which, through the provisions of ANCSA, represents the commercial interests of the village. "You can cross oil fields if you don't mind being harassed and treated like a criminal." And, while caribou might graze by a pump station and migrating geese flock to a nearby lake, these traditional hunting areas are now off-limits: shooting near the machinery and workers is of course forbidden.

"Some of the oil land is where we've always hunted, and we can't go there anymore," says Maggie Kovalsky, another member of Kuukpik's board of directors. "What will Conoco leave us? We can't eat the oil." Though she, Lampe, and others bear imposing titles, they're all ordinary citizens of this tight-knit, subsistence-oriented village. During our interview in Lampe's office, his young grandson toddles in to visit, decked in traditional mukluks and a wolverine-trimmed parka, its cloth shell emblazoned with Spiderman images. Lampe's corporate attire consists of jeans, a sweatshirt, and a ball cap. "I feel blessed to live here," he says. "It's a rich place, full of fish and animals." In the next breath, he expresses the Kuukpik Corpora-

RIGHT *By placing one end of the paddle to his ear and the other underwater, Iñupiaq whaler Dale Brower listens to beluga whales singing (springtime, Chukchi Sea).*

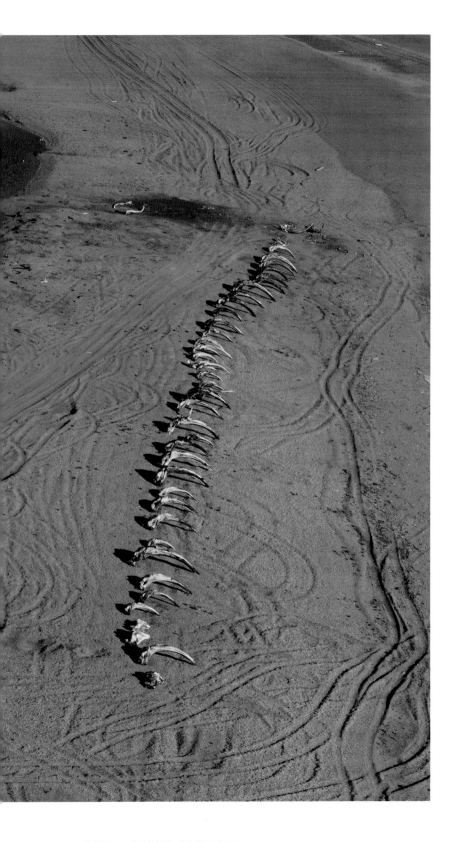

tion's ambitions to become more active players in oil development. They've recently purchased their own exploration rig. "We'll be Eskimo sheiks," Lampe grins, including himself in the joke.

As the conversation continues, Lampe shifts from polite chatting about Kuukpik's corporate goals to an increasingly heated stream of invective directed at ConocoPhillips. "They used to be respectful and helpful, but now that they have their permits, they don't care." He fumes about "discrimination so thick you could cut it with a knife" and ticks off a litany of grievances—everything from severe local air pollution, to lack of local hires (only 3 out of 380 jobs in the Alpine complex are currently filled by Nuiqsut residents), to an overdue natural-gas line that was to provide cheap energy to the village. And most important, the burgeoning development radiates outward to every point of the compass, far in excess of original assurances, an expansion that now includes plans for a bridge across the Colville River, part of a permanent road leading farther west into the NPRA. Adding insult to injury, Lampe explains, is that the planned road will bypass the village, reducing residents' economic opportunities. I gather that much (though certainly not all) of the local resentment stems from being cast pennies when they expected dollars. In any case, communication and cooperation between the village and ConocoPhillips, once a two-way street, has deteriorated into anger and frustration on both sides.

Still, every shareholder in the village, virtually every man, woman, and child, has just received their annual Kuukpik dividend check— $4,500 each, their share of Alpine. The money seems to scarcely dull the resentment percolating through the village; teenagers in the high school rail against oil, no doubt reflecting what they've heard at home. One Barrow official had warned me, "Asking the people of Nuiqsut about oil development right now is like asking someone how they feel in the middle of a root canal."

At least one Nuiqsut resident radiates no such angst. Sarah Kunaqnana sits on the couch in her comfortably cluttered plywood cabin. Despite her eighty-five years, her eyes are bright. And as she

LEFT *Bowhead whale jawbones lined up on Cross Island, along the Arctic coast, a traditional hunting area for the Iñupiat from Nuiqsut*

speaks in Iñupiaq, her voice is strong, her gestures expressive, though at times she wanders in her memories. With Lampe leaning in and translating, she tells me that she was born in 1921 on Cross Island, a whaling camp off the coast, and grew up as a nomad. "I still know every lake and pond and where to go on the ocean," she says. "My husband was a good traveler with dog team." They settled in the Colville River area in 1964 but still occasionally used the sod *iglu* her family had built near Prudhoe Bay—a house that was bulldozed flat with the coming of oil, to make room for the Deadhorse Hotel. "I sacrificed my land," she tells me. "Our people were raised not to be troublemakers."

Kunaqnana continues, "We're equal people, the oil companies and us. We should all have the opportunity of the land. It's good they use it." I can read from Lampe's face that he's as nonplussed as I am. But his manner is deferential, his voice soft as he continues to translate carefully. I suspect that Kunaqnana's true message was intended for Lampe, not me. I wonder if she's concerned that his outspoken opinions may result in backlashes by ConocoPhillips against the village—perhaps already have.

Asked if she has noticed any natural changes for the worse, Kunaqnana speaks emphatically. "The land is still the same, and it still provides. But too many people are working for wages. They're playing instead of hunting." Then she switches to English, her voice lilting. "Everyone always try to help each others. I never trouble how many years." As we take our leave, I reflect on the traditional Iñupiaq value of conflict avoidance and on a simpler time when the land itself was wealth enough—a past that seems impossibly distant.

THE RETURN FLIGHT FROM NUIQSUT to Barrow is first routed east to Deadhorse, at the Prudhoe epicenter. In light snow and nebulous darkness, we fly low along the coast, mile after mile of brightly lit oil fields stretching away—cities of never-sleeping pipe and thrumming machinery, a grid of profit and loss that links us all, set against the profundity of space. I wonder what a polar bear, traveling its solitary way out on the drifting ice, must think of those enclaves glittering in the Arctic winter night, defining a realm beyond its own perfectly honed genetic experience. Surely it notices, cocks its head and raises nostrils into the wind, catches the distant pulse of things alive and moving, the strange, thick scents. The white bear moves on, traversing the edge of ice and water, the edge between worlds.

PHOTO BY MARK KELLEY

Nick Jans is a longtime contributing editor to Alaska *magazine and a member of* USA Today's *board of editorial contributors. He has written seven books, including* The Grizzly Maze: Timothy Treadwell's Fatal Obsession with Alaska's Bears, A Place Beyond: Finding Home in Arctic Alaska, *and* Tracks of the Unseen. *He has published more than two hundred magazine articles and won a number of literary awards, most recently a 2006 Ben Franklin Award. He is also a professional photographer who specializes in wildlife and bush Alaska. Jans lived and taught school for twenty years in remote Native communities and currently makes his home in Juneau with his wife, Sherrie, three dogs, two parrots, and a varying array of wild critters that need a hand.*

Steven Kazlowski

PHOTOGRAPHER'S JOURNAL: POINT HOPE

It was mid-June and the snow had finally melted, but the ice was still hanging on tight to the land. I was on my way to meet my friend Tim Cook, flying over the northwest coast of Alaska. As I looked out the window of the plane, I could see the rich environment of land, ice, and water below.

Photographing in the Arctic is often filled with long periods of waiting—waiting for weather, waiting for animals, waiting for the right light—but these are always followed by times of excitement and wonder. This was one of those days. The weather was nice enough that we could see in all directions, and we were headed to a place I had never been before: Point Hope, one of the oldest Iñupiaq settlements in the Arctic. We turned south over Cape Lisburne, the northwesternmost point of Alaska and the North American continent, and I knew it wouldn't be long before we landed.

I was picked up at the strip by Tim's friend Larry Higbee. Larry had settled in the Arctic in the 1970s and married a Native woman; they'd had a child and adopted another. His first wife had long since passed away from cancer, his children were grown, and now he was remarried. Tim and I camped out on couches in Larry's living room, which doubles as an office for the Frontier freight department that he runs as the ticket agent.

The village was abuzz with four-wheelers coming and going from the ice along the southern coastal sandspit. The ice had stayed onshore late this season—a boon to the local hunters, as it allowed them to get on and off the ice to hunt. Without the onshore ice, the hunters needed a boat to get out to the pack ice, which was a more expensive proposition. Both the bearded and ringed seals were migrating through now. The bearded seal, a favorite prey of the polar bear, is equally loved by the Iñupiat. The meat is prized, and

LEFT *The Iñupiat use skins of the* ugruk *(bearded seal) to make* umiaks *and other structures.*

the boats used for spring whaling are made out of the skins.

Twenty-four hours a day, for 20 miles up and down the coast, the Iñupiat were hunting. I heard the sound of gunfire over and over. That night, Tim's friend Mike Dirks told us he had witnessed something he had never seen before: hundreds of seals up on the ice about a mile or two out. In the Arctic, there are always strange and wonderful things to see. The next day, Mike and a younger cousin took us out hunting.

Although a late-spring melt is a good thing for hunters, it is a dangerous time to be on the ice. At any moment, the ice could cut away from the coast and take everything on it along for the ride. The fog rolled in and lifted, rolled in and lifted all night; small shots of golden light pierced the clouds, illuminating the landscape. In open pools in the ice, seal heads popped up and tails slapped the water as the seals realized they were being watched. I had been on and around the ice for months now. I had seen the ice change from being locked solid to giving way to patches of open water, a sign that meant the heart of summer had arrived.

Mike finally got a ringed seal. The most difficult part about seal hunting is getting a hook into the animal after it has been shot, as the wounded or dead seal tends to sink fast. But Mike hooked his kill and pulled it up onto the ice. He was happy; he would eat the meat and use the skin for his artwork: Iñupiaq dolls made out of skins and fur.

It was raining hard now, and Tim and I went to Larry's house to sleep. We woke occasionally to the sounds of phones ringing and boxes coming and going. After a few hours of rest, we headed to the old village site: row after row of collapsed sod houses. The houses were made of whale-bone frames covered with sod and dirt. One was still partially standing; an older woman had lived in that house until the early 1970s—with an active phone line. There were two rooms: a front room where food was stored and a back room where people lived. This was the Alaskan Iñupiaq permanent style of

ABOVE *It is rare to see so many ringed seals together on the ice; note the dark exit holes.*

CLOCKWISE FROM TOP LEFT
A watchful ringed seal / Clouds and fog, changing angles of sunlight, and reflections off water and ice make for intriguing photographic conditions in the Arctic. / Russell Lane and his family take a break from hunting bearded seals (early summer, Point Hope, Alaska). / Iñupiaq hunter Mike Dirks with a ringed seal catch (summer, Chukchi Sea)

housing along the coast until the 1940s, when they began erecting wooden houses.

In the adjacent graveyard was an area of freestanding whale bones. Another area the size of a small football field was surrounded by a fence made out of all types of whale bones, with grave markers in the middle. Long ago, the Iñupiaq people would leave their dead above-ground on whale bones. When Christianity came to the area, the missionaries taught the Iñupiat to make a graveyard and put the dead belowground. But some people have gone back to using bone markers set outside of the Christian graveyard.

Tim had to leave, but I stayed on. I accompanied Mike, his wife, their small child, and a young nephew on a trip south, down the sandspit to Cape Thompson, 25 miles away in the Alaska Maritime National Wildlife Refuge. It's a beautiful place, with cliffs rising more than 1,000 feet above the sea. Tens of thousands of thick-billed and common murres fly in to and out from the cliffs, where they nest. My Iñupiaq friends call these birds Alaskan flying penguins. It was early in the season, and only a few had begun laying their light-blue speckled eggs.

Mike and his family eventually headed back to town, but I decided to camp on the beach for a few days. I found a nice spot near the base of the cliffs, collected some driftwood, and built a small fire. By the time I had settled in, it was the middle of the night,

but the sky was tinged gold by the midnight sun, which rested low on the horizon. As the fire slowly turned to glowing embers, I reflected on what I had seen during my time on the ice.

The fate of the thick-billed and common murres is likely similar to that of other regional species. The ice, although nearby this spring, has seasonally been receding farther and farther from shore, requiring the murres to travel longer distances to find their main food source, Arctic cod. Food sources for cod are also becoming scarcer because of the changes occurring in the water, which in turn reduces the number of cod that survive. Scientists have been finding that less-nutritious pollock have been increasing in place of the cod. The murres are losing more chicks each breeding season for want of a nutritious diet, and if these conditions continue, the birds' survival will be in question.

Morning arrived. I walked the edge of the beach to photograph the murres as they flew around the cliffs, and then I started climbing a cliff, hanging on tightly until I got to the top, more than 1,000 feet above the beach. It was hard to believe that some Iñupiat climb down from these clifftops to collect eggs. I lay down and took a nap, lulled by the sun's warmth, refreshed by a cooling breeze. When I awoke, the sun was high overhead. The landscape here is a combination of rounded and steep hills covered in tundra and vegetation, with a slip of beach at the base of the cliffs. I admired the views for some time before heading back down a less-steep slope. I stayed one more night and then turned toward the village on my borrowed four-wheeler.

I arrived back in town at about four in the morning and slept for a few hours, only to be wakened by Larry, who reminded me that it was the Fourth of July—the one day of the year that I could take pictures of the local residents without disturbing anyone in the community.

It was a clear blue-sky day of 40 degrees Fahrenheit, a summer's day in the Arctic. The parade included decorated four-wheelers, cars, and trucks carrying people costumed in a variety of traditional dress

CLOCKWISE FROM TOP LEFT
Fossilized walrus bones at the old village site outside Point Hope, Alaska. Before the Iñupiat moved here, a tribe believed to be closely related to the Navajo in Arizona lived here in the Arctic; they disappeared sometime after the Iñupiat arrived. Not much is known about these people except that they ate walruses, not whales. / This sod house in the old village outside Point Hope was last occupied in 1972, a vestige of ancient times that reflects the change of cultures. The two nails sticking up out of the whale jawbone were used for a phone hookup. The current village of Point Hope is the oldest settlement in North America. / A fence made out of bowhead whalebones of all kinds surrounds the graveyard. / Whalebones mark gravesites.

ABOVE *The cliffs at Cape Thompson, a rich habitat for nesting birds, including thick-billed and common murres*

ABOVE *From Cape Thompson, the coast extends north to Point Hope.*

OVERLEAF *Thick-billed and common murres on the ice at Cape Thompson*

and patriotic clothing, with American flags on display. The people were friendly and shy, reserved and outgoing. Everyone—young and old alike—participated in the celebration. It's common in Iñupiaq communities for even the elders to join in on activities that we in the Lower 48 might consider to be kids' games. A friend of mine from the area once emailed to say that she was waiting for her father, who was more than eighty years old, to come home from an Easter egg hunt! On this bright day, it seemed as if everyone just wanted to have fun.

The evening sky was beautiful, and by the next morning the ice had finally pulled off the coast to give way to the open ocean. Here the polar bears, bearded and ringed seals, walruses, and eider ducks pass by on their spring, summer, and fall migrations, and here the Iñupiaq people live, calling this place home, as they have always done, and waiting for the animals to pass by in the circle of life. Again I thought of the climate changes taking place—loss of sea ice and rising temperatures—and I saw in the warmth of the rising sun the danger that this sandspit, with all its abundant life, might one day disappear under the rising sea.

PRECEEDING PAGE *Common and thick-billed murres nesting on the cliffs*

LEFT *An Iñupiaq girl from Point Hope*

CLOCKWISE FROM TOP LEFT
Skin-boat races are part of the Iñupiaq celebration of Independence Day. / Moss campion / Point Hope's Fourth of July parade / Arctic poppies

We need the right policies—now—to ensure that solutions are deployed on the scale necessary to achieve deep reductions in global-warming pollution.

Frances Beinecke

A Climate for Change: Next Steps in Solving Global Warming

PEOPLE DON'T OFTEN TALK ABOUT global warming and hope in the same breath, but I feel hopeful about where we are headed. Yes, I have read the grave scientific reports, and I have seen the warning signs already blazing across the landscape: the diminished snowfalls that threaten our water supply, the intense wildfires that scorch our forests, the deadly heat waves that endanger our children and elderly. This is the moral issue of our time, a crisis that could endanger millions of people and profoundly degrade the earth. And yet I have also seen more-positive signs as well, signs revealing that American people finally understand they have the power to help stop global warming.

I saw one of these signs emerge from the Arctic. When people learned that polar bears are drowning because the sea ice is melting away beneath their feet, citizen activists took a stand. These majestic animals have evolved to thrive in the fiercest climate on earth, and yet suddenly they are struggling to survive. They sit at the top of the food chain, and yet many are now starving. The cause of their demise is clear: global warming is making the sea ice they depend on disappear at an alarming rate. Polar bears could become the first mammals to lose 100 percent of their habitat to global warming. And the powerful images of their struggles that have been transmitted around the world have mobilized the public.

People have a strong, visceral response to these images. They can see that global warming is already having a concrete and damaging impact on our world, and they have decided it has to stop. More than 500,000 Americans sent messages to the federal government—in just one ninety-day comment period in 2007—demanding that polar bears be protected under the Endangered Species Act. That almost doubled the public comments generated by any other

endangered species listing in U.S. history. In a stunning victory for polar bears and their advocates, the U.S. Fish and Wildlife Service proposed listing the polar bear as a threatened species, but will not issue its final decision until the end of 2007. If Fish and Wildlife fails to protect the bears, the Natural Resources Defense Council (NRDC) and the Center for Biological Diversity will sue the government, and we will mobilize citizen activists to protest.

It is our mission to force the government to listen to this overwhelming chorus demanding protection for polar bears. Time and again I have witnessed the power of citizen action. I have seen how people armed with passion and determination have stopped the clear-cutting of entire old-growth forests in Alaska, prevented the despoiling of gray whale nursing grounds in Mexico, and blocked efforts to make red-rock canyons in Utah into industrialized oil-drilling zones. If we apply the same citizen pressure to the challenge of global warming, we can make a profound difference.

We can do this because solutions do exist to stop global climate change. We have technologies in hand today that can cut greenhouse-gas emissions in half, but we must embrace them, and soon, to avert the worst damages to the planet.

The fastest and cheapest way to start reducing global-warming pollution is through energy efficiency, or doing more with less energy. The largest source of global-warming pollution in the United States comes from generating electricity, particularly from coal-fired power plants, but if we shift to using appliances and building practices that demand less electricity, we can dramatically cut carbon dioxide emissions.

Products on the market right now can help us do that. Today's refrigerators consume 75 percent less energy than those produced in the late 1970s, and dishwashers that meet the federal government's Energy Star efficiency guidelines use 50 percent less energy than

LEFT *The midnight sun over the frozen Chukchi Sea*

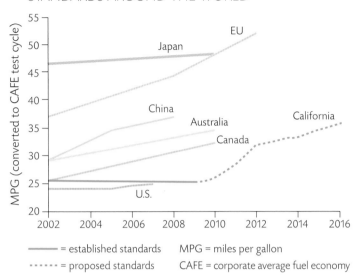

FUEL ECONOMY AND GHG EMISSION
STANDARDS AROUND THE WORLD

= established standards   MPG = miles per gallon

.... = proposed standards   CAFE = corporate average fuel economy

SOURCE: "COMPARISON OF PASSENGER VEHICLE FUEL ECONOMY AND GHG EMISSION
STANDARDS AROUND THE WORLD," BY AN AND SAUER, PEW CENTER ON
GLOBAL CLIMATE CHANGE, DECEMBER 2004

Figure 9. Burning fuel to power cars and trucks is the second-largest source of global-warming pollution in America, which lags behind many other industrialized nations in fuel-efficiency standards.

standard models. Home electronics are another area with great potential for energy reductions. There are more than 100 million computer monitors in use in U.S. homes and businesses, consuming almost 1 percent of the electricity used nationwide. In 2004, computer monitor manufacturers agreed, at NRDC's request, to set a more stringent performance standard for the popular flat-panel liquid crystal diode (LCD) monitors. As a result of these changes, the U.S. Environmental Protection Agency estimates that by 2010 the nation will save more than $14 billion in electricity bills and approximately 37.6 billion pounds of carbon dioxide—the equivalent of taking roughly 2.9 million cars off the road.

Imagine what we could accomplish if we make similar reductions across states and the entire country. California is pointing the way. Since the 1970s, California has enacted energy-efficiency standards

for appliances and buildings, and now the average California resident uses 40 percent less electricity than an American elsewhere—even as the state's population has exploded and its gross state product more than doubled in the past two decades. In 2004, California improved on its stellar record when its utilities agreed to provide $2 billion in efficiency incentives over three years. The program gives rebates ranging from $35 to $600 to people who buy energy-efficient appliances. The combined electricity and natural-gas savings will reduce carbon emissions by more than 9 million tons every year, the equivalent of taking 40 percent of the Bay Area's vehicles off the road.

Reducing our electricity use will provide deep reductions in carbon emissions, but we cannot solve global warming unless we make our cars more efficient as well. Burning fuel to power our cars and trucks is the second-largest source of global-warming pollution in America. In 2002, California took the bold step of passing the first law limiting carbon dioxide emissions from cars. Ten other states are following California's visionary lead. In response, U.S. and foreign automakers are suing those states to prevent these laws from taking effect, but rather than putting up roadblocks, they should offer consumers more-efficient cars. Automobiles can reach fuel efficiencies of 40 miles per gallon with improvements in conventional gasoline technology, and they can reach 55 miles per gallon with gasoline-electric hybrids. The best hybrids on the market today already reduce global-warming pollution and oil use by 50 percent compared to average cars—and they save money at the pump.

Efficient appliances, homes, and cars present tremendous opportunities for reducing global-warming pollution, but efficiency alone is not enough. The magnitude of global climate change is simply too great for us to solve by relying on one answer. We need also to shift to more-sustainable ways of powering our homes and cars.

America is beginning to tap the potential of renewable energy.

CLOCKWISE FROM TOP LEFT
The ice bends beneath the weight of a polar bear sow and her cubs (autumn, near the Arctic National Wildlife Refuge). / Staying close in a snowstorm during freeze-up; polar bears have a body temperature similar to our own, but under conditions that defy imagination (autumn, coastal plain, Arctic National Wildlife Refuge). / A polar bear in slushy ice during freeze-up (autumn, near the Arctic Refuge) / Sows defrost frozen whale meat in the water as cubs play.

Solar energy employs more than twenty thousand Americans in high-tech, high-paying jobs. Wind power is the fastest growing form of electricity generation in the United States, expanding at a rate of more than 20 percent per year. Thanks to the latest technology, wind power is now cost competitive with new coal- or gas-fired power plants. Large utilities, municipal power companies, and suburban developments see the value in renewables, but we need to make renewables a much larger portion of our energy-supply portfolio. Fortunately, twenty states have passed standards that require utilities to generate as much as 25 percent of the state's electricity demand from renewable sources. Now we need similar action on the federal level.

We also need similar incentives for developing renewable, clean-burning fuels. Biofuels—fuels made from plant materials—show great promise as a replacement for gasoline. Ethanol producers already make 5 million gallons of fuel a year, but America can do better, both in terms of how much we produce and how well we produce it. If we start by making our cars more efficient and by building less car-dependent, more livable communities, and then establish strict environmental standards to foster best practices for growing and making clean-burning fuels, we can dramatically reduce the global-warming pollution generated by transportation. Aggressive action between now and 2015 would position the United States to virtually eliminate our demand for gasoline by 2050.

This is not the stuff of science fiction. The biofuels industry relies on real-world technologies that are improving by leaps and bounds. With technological advances that we could deploy over the next ten years, we could produce biofuels at prices competitive with gasoline and diesel, and cars that give drivers a choice between gasoline, biofuels, and electricity are being developed today. By 2050,

CLOCKWISE FROM TOP LEFT
Immature snowy owl (springtime, near Point Barrow, National Petroleum Reserve–Alaska) / Endangered Steller's eiders on summer tundra; only a few hundred remain (summer, near Point Barrow, National Petroleum Reserve–Alaska). / A golden eagle / A spectacled eider takes flight over a freshwater lake (summer, near Point Barrow, National Petroleum Reserve–Alaska).

RIGHT *An Arctic fox in its summer coat looks something like the red fox, an increasing competitor for habitat in the Arctic (Prudhoe Bay, Alaska).*

CURRENT RENEWABLE ENERGY RESOURCES

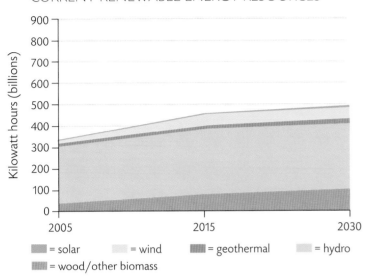

SOURCE: "IMPACTS OF A 15 PERCENT RENEWABLE PORTFOLIO STANDARD," ENERGY INFORMATION ADMINISTRATION, U.S. DEPARTMENT OF ENERGY, JUNE 2007

POTENTIAL RENEWABLE ENERGY RESOURCES

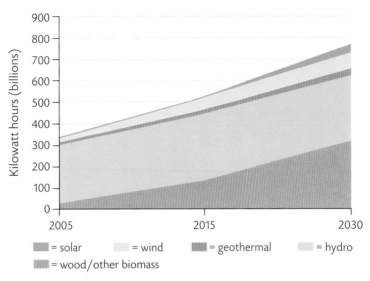

SOURCE: "IMPACTS OF A 15 PERCENT RENEWABLE PORTFOLIO STANDARD," ENERGY INFORMATION ADMINISTRATION, U.S. DEPARTMENT OF ENERGY, JUNE 2007

Figure 10. America is beginning to tap the potential of renewable energy resources.

Figure 11. Yet we can make renewables a much larger portion of our energy supply; here is what it would look like if 15 percent of U.S. electricity sales were derived from renewable energy resources.

biofuels—especially those known as cellulosic biofuels—could reduce our greenhouse gases by 1.7 billion tons per year. That's equal to more than 80 percent of current transportation-related emissions.

Even if we dramatically improve our energy efficiency and renewable power, the plain truth is that coal-fired power plants will be with us for a long time. Coal generates more than half of the electricity we use in the United States, and it is the most carbon-intense form of energy in use. China is building the equivalent of 2 large coal-fired power plants per week, while U.S. developers are planning to build 150 new plants in the near future. Power plants have a long life span—if we build new coal plants with dirty, nineteenth-century technologies, we lock ourselves into high levels of global-warming pollution for five or six decades.

We can instead choose a twenty-first-century alternative. There is no such thing as "clean coal," but we can generate the power we need by using a cleaner process that captures the carbon dioxide from coal and disposes of it deep underground. The most economi-

cal way to do this today is by turning the coal into a gas, stripping off the carbon (and storing it underground), and then using the resulting clean hydrogen to produce power. Each of these steps is used in the United States today, although not always at the same plant. In 2006, BP (British Petroleum) and the Edison Mission Group announced plans to build the country's first coal-fired plant to combine all three technologies. The plant, in Carson, California, will capture and store 90 percent of its carbon dioxide emissions. A project like this requires a larger initial investment than building a conventional coal plant, but developers are beginning to realize that mandatory caps on carbon emissions are around the corner, and if they don't build cleaner plants now, they will pay for the dirty carbon pollution later.

Indeed, all Americans pay for the damage caused by coal-powered electricity. With its underground mining accidents, mountaintop removal and strip mining, transportation of coal across the nation, and toxic emissions released when coal is burned, the coal fuel cycle

ABOVE *Sow and cub in the water (autumn, coastal plain, Arctic National Wildlife Refuge)*

ABOVE *A boar among driftwood (coastal plain, Arctic National Wildlife Refuge)*

is powerfully destructive. That's why at the same time as we in the United States begin to address coal power's global-warming legacy, we must also tackle its other environmentally degrading side effects.

Energy-efficient cars and appliances, biofuels, wind power, state-of-the-art coal plants—all of these solutions to global warming exist now, and increasingly, people are demanding them. They are putting their consumer muscle behind greener products, such as hybrid cars. While sport utility vehicle (SUV) sales are plummeting and Detroit's Big Three automakers—General Motors, Ford, and the Chrysler Group—hover on the brink of bankruptcy, Toyota's hybrid Prius was named *Motor Trend* magazine's Car of the Year in 2004, and customers sign up for six-month waiting lists to get these hybrid cars.

But people are also asking more from their politicians. When California considered passing the most ambitious law in the nation to limit statewide global-warming pollution, religious leaders, business owners, members of environmental justice groups, and thousands of online activists barraged their assembly members with support for the bill. It passed in September 2006, and now every major global-warming polluter in California must follow strict limits on greenhouse-gas emissions.

Knowing that people want these solutions gives me hope about our ability to stop global warming, but I also feel a sense of urgency. Scientists say we need to turn the corner on global warming within ten years to prevent dangerous impacts from becoming inevitable. Each year that passes without our tackling global warming head-on makes solving the problem more difficult and expensive. We simply have to act now to make these solutions more widespread.

People can make a difference in their own lives; we can all take many simple steps to reduce our energy and oil use (see the following sidebars). But the single most important action we can take is to pressure our leaders to address global warming now. It's up to all of us to increase the heat on our elected officials: we need the right policies—and we need them now—to ensure that solutions are deployed on the scale necessary to achieve deep reductions in global-warming pollution.

RIGHT *A large sow, fat from whale blubber (coastal plain, Arctic National Wildlife Refuge)*

In December 2006, scientists from the National Center for Atmospheric Research warned that if we fail to do this, all of the summer sea ice in the Arctic could be gone by 2040, and the polar bears could disappear along with it. But we will lose far more than these majestic creatures. Wallace Stegner wrote in his famous 1960 "Wilderness Letter" that you do not have to travel to a wilderness area to understand that it is worth saving: simply knowing that such a wild sanctuary exists is enough to create what he called "a geography of hope." The same is true for wild animals. Most Americans will never see a polar bear outside of a zoo, and yet hundreds of thousands of people have taken action to protect the bears. These people are taking a stand for glorious, untamed nature. And they are taking a stand for hope in a future safe from global warming. We should join them.

Frances Beinecke is president of the Natural Resources Defense Council (NRDC), one of the nation's most influential environmental action groups, which uses law, science, and the support of 1.2 million members and online activists to ensure a safe and healthy environment for all living things. Beinecke has been with the NRDC for more than thirty years, serving as executive director from 1998 through 2005. She received her bachelor's degree from Yale College and a master's degree from the Yale School of Forestry and Environmental Studies. Beinecke co-chairs the Leadership Council of the School of Forestry, serves on the advisory board of Yale's Institute for Biospheric Studies and the board of the World Resources Institute, and is a member of the steering committee of the Energy Future Coalition.

LEFT *Polar bears are powerful swimmers, but they do best in the calm, protected waters of leads among the pack ice; as the pack ice dwindles and they must swim farther and farther to reach it, they struggle in large expanses of open water in the stormy northern seas (summer, Arctic Ocean).*

ABOVE *Sow and cub playing in slushy ice*

ABOVE *Pressure ridges in summer (Chukchi Sea)*

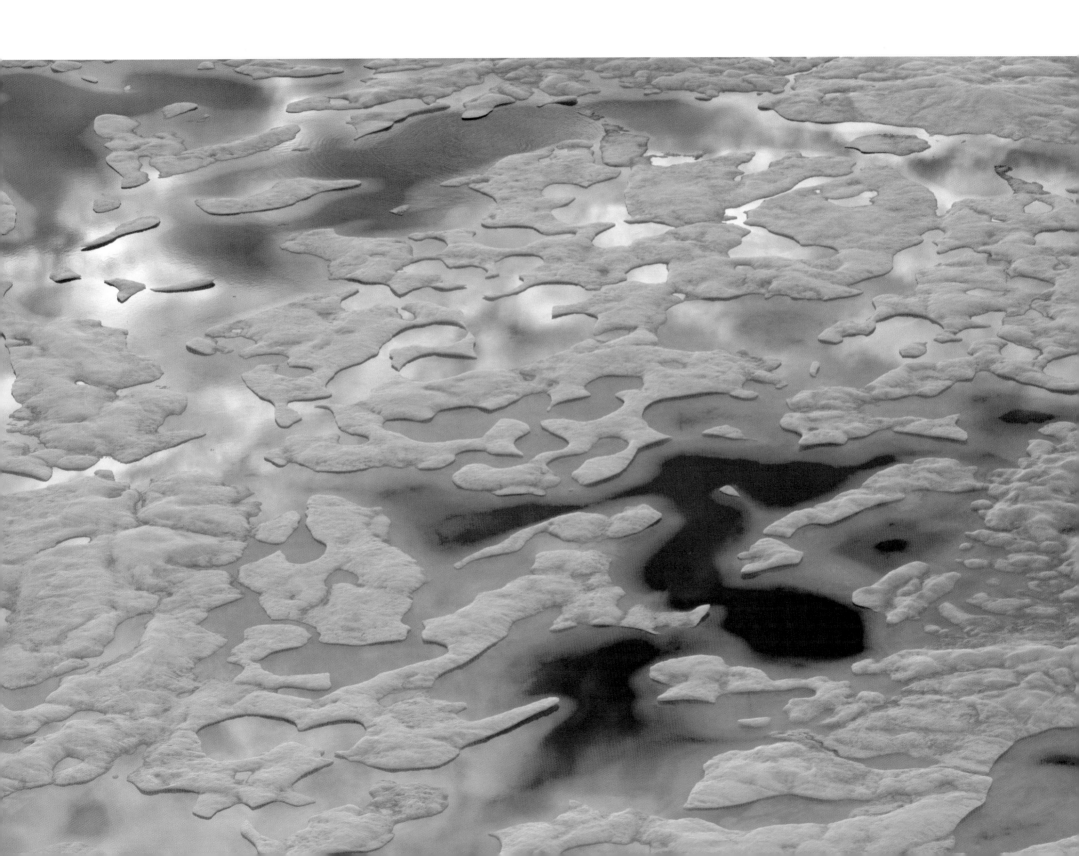

POSITIVE CHANGE BEGINS WITH YOU. TODAY.

Polar bears could use your help.

So could a lot of other life forms, including humans. Here are ways that you can make a difference in the polar bears' future—without living in guilt, in fear, or in a shivering, dark preindustrial cave. To prevent the planet from warming beyond the point where polar bears can survive, everybody can initiate a range of simple, practical, and effective actions to reduce greenhouse-gas emissions.

Start by observing your routines as if you had an energy-detecting device that displays the amount of energy consumed (or saved) because of a hundred decisions you make daily: driving to the store, leaving your computer on overnight, choosing a new appliance or car, setting the furnace thermostat. Every time you turn on your ignition or flip on a light switch, you contribute another feather to the atmosphere's down parka. But if each person makes even small changes, and those are multiplied over thousands and millions of fellow humans, the collective transformation will steamroll through society, drive the marketplace, and force political action. Ultimately, the planet itself will respond to our concerted efforts. Here are some suggestions and resources:

Support polar bear advocacy: Contribute to a wildlife organization such as World Wildlife Fund *(www.panda.org/polarbears)* or Polar Bears International *(www.polarbearsinternational.org)*. Groups such as these disseminate alerts and updates about how polar bears are faring, both politically and biologically, and can provide concrete examples of ways to help.

Tell your politicians how you feel: Make the future of the planet a top-priority voting issue. A handwritten letter or telephone call to your elected officials, whether a city councilperson or the president of the United States, makes a bigger impact than emails or petitions.

Tell them the changes you have already made in your household, and ask them to take climate change seriously. Vote for candidates who promote innovation and reform in the energy sector, including raising efficiency standards for automobile makers (possibly the most effective way to make a national impact). Vote against candidates who resist change or deny that the problem exists. To find contact information for your elected representatives, look at the website of Congress.org, a nonpartisan organization that promotes civic participation, and type in your zip code in the "Take Action" section *(www.congress.org/congressorg/home)*.

Think planet, not nation: Climate change is affecting every continent, but the human-driven causes of global warming can be largely attributed to the industrialized world's prolific use of fossil fuels. The United States has 5 percent of the world's population and produces about 25 percent of the world's carbon emissions. What we do and don't do to change that equation will tip the balance of the planet's future. Leadership is best done by example.

Be a spark plug in your community: Many states, counties, and cities are already showing the way with cost-effective efficiency measures, including purchasing fleets of hybrids or vehicles that run on renewable fuels, retrofitting community lighting, and installing more-effective heating systems in schools and government buildings. Almost every improvement in efficiency is good for a community's bottom line. See U.S. mayors' suggestions for best practices at the website of the U.S. Conference of Mayors *(http://usmayors.org/climateprotection)*. Sometimes the only impediment to sensible action is finding citizens to take the lead.

Establish a personal benchmark and start improving on it: Understand your own carbon imprint by logging on to *www.carbonfootprint.com,* and see where you could start making incremental improvements. (A carbon footprint, which indicates the amount of carbon dioxide emitted through combustion of fossil fuels, is a

LEFT *Summer evening aerial of ice (Chukchi Sea, near the National Petroleum Reserve–Alaska)*

representation of the effect of human activities on the climate in terms of the total amount of greenhouse gases produced.) For an excellent overview of the issue and a comprehensive look at where you can make effective changes, check out the David Suzuki Foundation *(www.davidsuzuki.org/Climate_Change)*. This Canadian foundation's website is a wealth of scientific background and practical information.

Use less gasoline: Quite simply, drive less and do it with a more fuel-efficient car. Your choice of vehicle is a great place to start reducing emissions. A person who drives a less efficient sport utility vehicle rather than an average passenger car will, over the course of a year, use more energy than if he left his refrigerator door open for six years, according to Daniel Becker of the Sierra Club. You can buy a hybrid, consolidate your chores into one driving trip, establish car-free days, keep your car tuned and the tires inflated, ride a bus, carpool, or look into sharing a car *(www.carsharing.net, www.flexcar.com, or www.zipcar.com)*.

Efficiency, efficiency, efficiency: In almost every case, saving energy and reducing greenhouse-gas emissions will save you money. Most state and regional energy companies will conduct a free energy audit of your home. Call your utility company to see where you're leaking energy—and emitting carbon dioxide. You can also conduct a do-it-yourself energy assessment at the Home Energy Saver website *(http://hes.lbl.gov)*. Meanwhile, turn off lights, chargers, and appliances when not in use; replace incandescent bulbs with compact fluorescents; lower the thermostat in winter by a couple degrees and raise it a couple in summer. Caulk your windows and buy window coverings. Weatherstrip your doors. Turn down your water heater to 120 degrees Fahrenheit, install low-flow showerheads and faucets. Check out the Environmental Protection Agency's Energy Star program

LEFT *Curious polar bears check out the photographer (coastal plain, Arctic National Wildlife Refuge)*

(*www.energystar.gov*) for more tips. Baby steps are fine. They add up.

Buy smarter, consume less, reduce, reuse, recycle: The to-do list here is long, from buying locally grown fruits and vegetables in season to taking fewer airplane trips and planning vacations closer to home. Buy items in bulk or in recyclable containers, and buy recycled products. Check the energy rating of appliances you buy (look for the Energy Star label), and don't buy what you don't need. Everything requires energy to manufacture and transport.

Move to renewables: Many utilities offer the option to pay a little more for "green" power, often from wind. Think about installing solar collectors on your roof, either to generate electricity (using photovoltaic cells) or to directly heat your hot water. With tax breaks and improved technology, these systems will pay for themselves in relatively short order, depending on your needs and your location. In some cases, payback periods are as short as a few years. One place to start learning more is at the American Solar Energy Society's website (*www.ases.org/index.htm*).

Become carbon neutral: Many companies now offer to offset individuals' carbon emissions by investing in renewable power and efficiency projects, such as planting carbon dioxide–absorbing trees or encouraging new technologies that promise a more carbon-neutral world. Carbon offsets have been criticized as a lazy alternative to making vital lifestyle changes (including those listed above). Even the most generous contributions to carbon-offset programs will not substitute for reducing your carbon emissions, but they can keep the carbon-reduction effort rolling. Think about investing in renewable energy and "green" businesses. You may also choose some of the offset options in the accompanying "Go Carbon Neutral" list, but also consider finding ways to make local impacts in your community: buy your neighbors some compact fluorescent bulbs and help to install them, contribute extra to your local utility's green-energy program for those who can't afford the extra cost, or research other effective carbon-offset programs. For one overview of such programs, download Clean Air–Cool Planet's consumer guide (*www.cleanair-coolplanet. org/ConsumersGuidetoCarbonOffsets.pdf*).

Vice President Dick Cheney once remarked that conservation was, at best, a "personal virtue" and not the government's responsibility. While many disagree with him on his second point, his first should not be dismissed easily. These days, with what we know about why the planet is warming, conservation is as much a personal virtue as courage, love, fairness, honesty, and generosity. It is as vital as treating thy neighbor as thyself, caring for people less fortunate than you, and behaving in a civilized society according to the rule of law.

Across the history of human cultures, there exists no higher personal virtue than to provide for our legacy—for our children and grandchildren. Their future is in peril, and it is time for each of us to do something to reverse or slow the ominous trend lines. Today.

—Daniel Glick

GO CARBON NEUTRAL

- The Canadian David Suzuki Foundation has an excellent, comprehensive, step-by-step list of actions that individuals can take: *www.davidsuzuki.org/Climate_Change/What_You_Can_Do /carbon_neutral.asp*.
- So does the Natural Resources Defense Council: *www.nrdc.org/globalWarming/default.asp*.
- See Al Gore's film *An Inconvenient Truth* and links to carbon-offset programs: *www.climatecrisis.net*.
- For buying carbon offsets, see the green directory and comprehensive comparison of carbon-offset companies at EcoBusinessLinks: *www.ecobusinesslinks.com/carbon_offset_wind_ credits_carbon_reduction.htm*.
- Here are a few companies offering carbon offsets: *www.carbonfund.org*, *www.terrapass.com*, *www.nativeenergy.com*.

ABOVE *Snowy owls: two juveniles and one adult*

CLOCKWISE FROM TOP LEFT
A wary sow with cubs watches another bear walk by (autumn, coastal plain, Arctic National Wildlife Refuge). / Playtime includes sledding (summer, Chukchi Sea). / An adult and subadult play (autumn, coastal plain, Arctic National Wildlife Refuge). / Walking on the pack ice (autumn, coastal plain, Arctic National Wildlife Refuge)

Photographer's Notes

Photographing in the Arctic is incredibly difficult due to extreme weather conditions. When conditions are good—some sunlight and relatively clear sky—the daylight can be amazing. Generally, 50–70 percent of time the weather is terrible—severely cold temperatures, piercing winds, snowy whiteouts, or ground fog—and it's not uncommon for weather to be bad 90 percent of the time! You can spend weeks up there and get only a day or two of good conditions; therefore, it is not a place you can fly into and quickly photograph what you're looking for.

Up until 2005, my 35mm camera equipment included a Nikon F100 and an N90S as a backup. I made the move to digital to get better photos, enabling me to shoot in less light, see immediate results, and make necessary corrections. Overall I have the ability to produce better images using a Nikon D2X as my main camera body and a D200 as a backup. The lithium batteries made specifically for the D2X are built better for cold weather and frigid temperatures and are stronger and longer lasting that the D200's lithium batteries.

The lenses I use include the following: 80–200mm (used quite a lot for wildlife), 500mm f4 manual, 105mm f2.8 (macro lens for flowers), 12–24mm f4 wide-angle lens, and a 28–70mm. I do not use filters. Prior to going digital, my use of 35mm film included the various Fuji Velvia, Sensia, and Provia films. I download images from my D2X daily to Smart Disks made by Micro Direct International.

In photographing in the Arctic, it is imperative yet difficult to keep equipment warm when temperatures are often below zero and there is fog and ice.

For shelter, I purchased the sturdy Arktika Arctic Oven tent and a stove from Alaska Tent and Tarp. I had them cut in custom windows, so when I needed to photograph out of the tent, I had several locations for my lens. I used ice screws purchased from climbing shops in Seattle to reliably hold down the tent and tarp in screaming winds of up to 60 miles per hour. In minus 25 to 60 degree Fahrenheit temperatures outside, the temperature in the tent would be just above or below 0 degrees F. When there was wood to burn in the stove, I could get the inside temperature up to 50–60 degrees F.

Gear and clothing need to operate in extreme cold when you're traveling and camping out along the Arctic coast or on the pack ice. I found a sleeping bag with a –60 degree F rating that I couldn't pass up, from Wiggy's Outdoor Gear in Anchorage, Alaska. I also purchased their Antarctic parka, bib, and mittens made from the same materials; I was happy I did this, as they have kept me warm. Wiggy's also created custom gear bags for me to hold sensitive photographic equipment (for instance, Smart Disks with stored images), to keep it from freezing. The primary ingredient they use for insulation is Lamilite (you can read more at *www.wiggys.com*). Outdoor Research in Seattle and Patagonia generously provided waterproof and windproof hardshell and softshell jackets and pants, fleece, wool and capilene thermals, hats, gloves, goosedown sleeping pads, and much-needed gear bags—essential quality items that I could not have lived without in the Arctic.

It takes a strong personality to work in the Arctic. You must be level headed and realize that failure is a constant reality. Success is rare, so you've got to make the most of it when it happens, but plan on failure so you can cope when it inevitably occurs.

I hope that reading this book and seeing my photographs is as rewarding for you as it was for me to bring these images to you and help make this book a reality. To see more of my work, please visit my website at *www.lefteyepro.com*.

—*Steven Kazlowski*

LEFT *Ice formed by wind and waves at the edge of a lead (Chukchi Sea)*

Resources

We hope that this book has inspired you to take action on behalf of the polar bears of the Arctic. As the effects of global climate change continue to become apparent, your voice is increasingly important. Many other wildlife species are also being affected, too, and you can help change this.

The news on the changing climate and its impact on the polar bear and its Arctic habitat becomes more urgent as each new scientific report is officially released to the public. Although every effort has been made to reflect the most up-to-date information in this publication, the nature of the problem is complex, highly volatile, and evolving rapidly. The principles and foundational information are timeless, but the details and time lines are subject to change beyond our current understanding. To obtain the latest scientific information on the topic of the Arctic environment, impacts to the polar bear, the health and biodiversity of the region, and what you can do as a citizen to become engaged in creating solutions, consult the many online resources, including the following resource sites—featuring those of our sponsoring partners.

Hundreds of organizations, businesses, and foundations that advocate for protecting the environment are working to educate the public and find solutions to ensure a healthy planet. Below are some organizations from which you can obtain more information about conservation issues, climate change, and polar bears. We encourage you to familiarize yourself with the issues and the organizations. Many depend on membership donations and volunteers to support their work. Contact them to find out how you can become involved.

* The Alaska Wilderness League and Natural Resources Defense Council are sponsoring organizations for *The Last Polar Bear* book and public outreach.

Advocacy Organizations

Alaska Conservation Foundation
www.akcf.org

Alaska Wilderness League*
www.alaskawild.org

Center for Biological Diversity
www.biologicaldiversity.org

Defenders of Wildlife
www.defenders.org

League of Conservation Voters
www.lcv.org

National Wildlife Federation
www.nwf.org

Natural Resources Defense Council*
www.polarbearSOS.org; www.nrdc.org

Sierra Club
www.sierraclub.org

The Wilderness Society
www.tws.org/ourissues/arctic

The Wildlife Conservation Society
www.wcs.org

World Wildlife Fund
*www.panda.org/polarbear.org,
www.worldwildife.org*

Alaska Native Organizations

Alaska Native Science Commission
www.nativescience.org

Arctic Slope Regional Corporation
www.asrc.com/home/home.asp

Gwich'in Steering Committee
www.gwichinsteeringcommittee.org

Kuukpik Corporation
www.kuukpik.com

North Slope Borough
www.co.north-slope.ak.us

Educational and Scientific Organizations

The Alliance for Climate Protection
www.climateprotect.org

Arctic Climate Impact Assessment Group
An Arctic Tale
www.allmovie.com/cg/avg.dll

Center for Global Change and Arctic
System Research
www.cgc.uaf.edu

Climate Arc
www.climateark.org/links

Climate Change Education
climatechangeeducation.org

David Suzuki Foundation
www.davidsuzuki.org

Earth Day Network
www.earthday.net

Ecumenical Earth, World Council
of Churches
www.wcc-coe.org/wcc/what/jpc/ecearth-climatechange.html

Environmental Literacy Council
www.enviroliteracy.org

The Globe Program, the National Center
for Atmospheric Research
www.globe.gov

Goddard Space Flight Center, NASA
icesat.gsfc.nasa.gov

Intergovernmental Panel on Climate
Change
www.ipcc.ch

International Polar Year
www.ipy.org

National Ice Core Laboratory, National
Science Foundation
nicl.usgs.gov

The Pew Center on Global
Climate Change
www.pewclimate.org

Polar Bears International
www.polarbearsinternational.org

The Sundance Channel—The Green
www.sundancechannel.com/thegreen

Union of Concerned Scientists
www.ucsusa.org

United Nations Framework Convention on
Climate Change Kyoto Protocol
unfccc.int/kyoto_protocol/items/2830.php

U.S. Conference of Mayors
usmayors.org/climateprotection

Woods Hole Oceanographic Institution
www.whoi.edu

The World Conservation Union
www.iucn.org

World Resources Institute
www.wri.org

Public Lands / Managers

Alaska Department of Fish and Game
www.adfg.state.ak.us

Alaska Maritime National Wildlife Refuge
alaskamaritime.fws.gov

Arctic National Wildlife Refuge
arctic.fws.gov

Canadian Wildlife Service
www.cws-scf.ec.gc.ca

NOAA Climate Program Office
www.climate.noaa.gov

U.S. Department of the Interior
www.doi.gov

U.S. Fish and Wildlife Service
www.fws.gov

U.S. Geological Survey
www.usgs.gov

Reduce Energy Use, Calculate Your Impact

Alternative Fuels Data Center,
U. S. Department of Energy
www.eere.energy.gov/afdc

Carbon Fund
www.carbonfund.org

Climate Friendly
www.climatefriendly.com

Energy Star
www.energystar.gov

Environmental Defense
www.fightglobalwarming.com

E-Rideshare
www.e-rideshare.com

Public Transportation: Wherever
Life Takes You
www.publictransportation.org

TerraPass
www.terrapass.com

Wikipedia Energy Portal
en.wikipedia.org/wiki/Portal:Energy

LEFT *Edge of an open lead in ice fog, midnight sun (springtime, Chukchi Sea)*

Acknowledgments

From Steven Kazlowski

Fifteen years ago I decided that photographing wildlife and nature was to be my life's work, and this book is a selection of those images from the Arctic. Without the ongoing support of strangers and friends, my work would have come to an end a long time ago—so much so that, at times, the images I make don't feel solely my own.

First and foremost I want to thank the love of my life, Sunny Coulson, who has accompanied me every step of the way, making sense of chaos for the last seven years.

Larry Wagner, my Anchorage backyard mechanic, kept me on the road for pennies in old trucks that led me up the Dalton Highway and into the Arctic. There I met Bill Morris, who took me under his wing and then tossed me out in the direction of a small Native village in eastern Arctic Alaska.

Ed Traynor welcomed me into the Waldo Arms Hotel and handed me over to bush pilot and hotel owner Walt Audi and his partner, Merylin Traynor. These three people have made me a part of their family and have given me a home in the Arctic for close to a decade. They are the main reason my work on the great white bear has been possible.

My Iñupiaq friend Fred Kaleak spent countless hours showing me who the polar bears were. Kent Sims pulled me off of the sandspit and kept me out of the ocean. Daniel Akootchook and Papa Taga-rook have my deep appreciation for hours of Iñupiaq lessons and stories of the old ways, which were not that long ago.

A special thank-you to Jack Kayotuk, who decided years ago to be part of a project he felt was important. He was always there, first to take me out on the coastal ice, then to consider this project his own and dedicate countless unpaid hours to making sure I was on the ice or in a boat out on the water. If not for his philosophy of helping others when he could, many of these images would not have been created. Jack has become a close buddy in life.

Jack took me on a snow machine ride to find a polar bear den three years after we had first talked about it, and returned with me in the spring to wait for the bears to emerge. He let me travel with him and Alice Faith to Herschel Island, a place of bright and dark magic where I met these kind folks: Mervin Joe, Lee John Meyook, Jonas Meyook, Phillip Ross, Dale Semple. Thanks as well to Ronnie "Frenchy" Drouin, a bush pilot who truly stands alone among all bush pilots. Bruce Inglangasak patiently sat with me and took me out on the land over and over again, showing me the many secrets of this country.

The photographer Subhankar Banerjee suggested this project and introduced me to Helen Cherullo, publisher at The Mountaineers Books. His *Arctic National Wildlife Refuge: Seasons of Life and Land* set the stage for other works, such as this one, to come alive. His artistry and his generosity in sharing the playing field will always touch me deeply, and I hope to emulate his example.

Helen Cherullo has backed me and this project every step of the way. There will never be a publisher of this caliber again. She truly believes in a better world and hope for tomorrow and gives it her all.

I also extend thanks to the rest of the book project staff: Christine Clifton-Thornton, my trusty barometer who fine-tuned my rawness and created a beautifully flowing work and who, when this book was short an Iñupiaq voice, found time on her own dime to jump on a plane and spend a few days with the well-respected elder whaler Arnold Brower Sr.; also Kathleen Cubley, Kris Fulsaas, Deb Easter, Julie Van Pelt, Ingrid Emerick, Kerry Smith, Rita Cipalla, Laura Case, Jane Jeszeck, and others who worked on this project.

I thank my many friends in Kaktovik: the elders Roy and Isaac Akootchook; Lillian Akootchook; Clara Apayauq Akootchook, who leads the next generation of Iñupiat into the future; Postmaster General Dave Tetreau; school cook Sherrie Wolf; and many others, among them Glenda Lord, Sonny Lampey and the Lampey family, Eve and Loren Ahlers, Nora Jane Burns, Joe and Lucy Kaleak, T. K. Kaleak and the Kaleak family for their love of *nanuq*, Lon Sonsalla, Annie Tikluk, Russell Tagarook, John Tagarook, Susan Gordon, Charlie and Marjorie Brower, Luann Balcom, Felicia Brower, the Brower family for food and companionship along the coast, Roland Kayotuk, Robert and Jane Thompson, Thomas Gordon and his wife for the good meals at Demarcation Bay, Robert and Eva Arey, Charlie Arey, and Fred Arey for boat help.

In Barrow, Scott Wolgemuth and his wife Tina gave me a place to stay. Scott handed me off to Bob Lozano, whom I spent all of twenty minutes with before he gave me a snow machine and sled to use and took me out to the Hopson I whale crew. Captain Chuck Hopson welcomed me and said that people needed to see what would be lost. The rest of the crew—Curtis Hopson, Perry Hopson, Stacey Hopson, Richard Bodfish, Freddy Hopson, Clyde Ahmaogak, Dean Tucker—let me sleep in their tent, and they and the captain let me come back in following seasons to live on the ice and be at the leads' edge. Richard Glenn and Craig George took the time to talk with me, giving me insight as to how the pack ice works and what it is. Martin Boardman and James C. Wolgemuth let me live with them in their bunkhouse, Tim Wolgemuth and Bill Nyehle helped me out, and Jim and Teresa Junkins provided me with bike transportation and a few laughs. I am grateful to the Brower whalers, especially Arnold Brower Sr. for adding his voice and to Eugene Brower, Dale Brower, Frederick Brower, Price Brower, and the Brower crews for letting me stay out on the ice with them. Thanks to the ABC crew, Harry Brower, and the Alaska Whaling Commission for letting me photograph their whale, and to Geoff and Marie Carroll for letting me photograph them and their sled-dog team on the pack ice.

In Point Hope, Tim Cook of Alaska ATV Adventures introduced me to his friends and to a truly amazing place. Russell and Andrea Lane took me hunting and let me stay at their home. Mike Dirks let me tag along seal hunting and showed me Cape Thompson. Larry Higbee gave me a place to stay and a four-wheeler to get around on.

The help of biologists has also proved invaluable. Tony and Tracy Fischbach have lent much support over many years, from housing to maps to helping me get into the field. Chad Davis let me come along on a walrus cruise. Steve Amstrup and Geoffrey York worked with the book's essayists and contributed scientific information about polar bears. Ian Stirling, longtime Canadian polar bear biologist, whom I met on Herschel Island, gave me valuable insight into the bears and their changing environment. Brendan Kelly and his team of scientists have also shared information, and thanks to George Divoky and his lifelong research on Cooper Island.

I have been fortunate to work with such high-caliber writers: Ted Roosevelt, whom I met only briefly several years ago in Kaktovik, lent his public voice and gave me the thumbs-up on continuing my work in the Arctic. Dan Glick sat with me for four days in a truck on a sand-spit and constructively tore the imagery of this project apart to guide me in thinking critically about what was needed visually. Richard Nelson offered kind words and, more specifically, his knowledge of and commitment to the people and environment of the Arctic. I also thank Frances Beinecke for her imperative work on global warming and polar bear protection at the Natural Resources Defense Council, and Nick Jans and Charles Wohlforth for their hard work and heartfelt essays. Laurie David, Bill McKibben, and Gus Speth generously made time to review and comment on the manuscript.

Thanks to my sponsors: John Detrick, Outdoor Research, Patagonia, Southwest Wind Power, and Wiggys. Tom and Sonya Campion and Marlyn Twitchell of the Campion Foundation also provided support, as did Ellen Ferguson and the Hugh and Jane Ferguson Foundation; Chris and Mary Troth; Ann and Ron Holz; and Carolyn Moore and the George L. Shields Foundation. John Nuhn and Mark Wexler of *National Wildlife* magazine published

my work from the Arctic coast, giving me financial support.

Peter McNally kept me technologically up to date. Jeremy Burgess made my images into postcards and kept the supply stocked so I could bring in enough small change to keep going. Thanks also to anyone who's ever bought one of my cards, to all my stock agencies and their staff for helping me along in an ever-changing business, to my sales rep Ken Mills, to Ken Crandall of the Mailbox in Seattle, to Molly and John Van Norstrand of Fast Frame in Seattle, to Drs. Perry Jones and Neil Bryant, and to Patty Stith and the Education through Cultural and Historical Organizations (ECHO) Project in Barrow.

Steve Nourse, Andreas Keiling, Yva Momatiuk and John Eastcott, Tom and Pat Leeson, Florian and Emil Shultz, John and Cindy Schweider, Steve MacAulay, and Greg Syverson have shared their years of experience, both in the field and in the business of a very difficult occupation.

My parents instilled in me a wildness in my youth that made me want to explore the far reaches of the earth—namely, the Arctic. Michael Kazlowski gave me a connection to my own past. And many friends have supported and encouraged me over the years in the way of housing and meals, advice and laughs: Bob and Emma Audi; Bart Baum; Joy Beatty; Robyn Becker; Martha Equinox; Jamey and Lenka Gayton; Shelley Gill; Ed Gollin; Darren Hackett; Scott Henry; Dr. Kathleen Halloran, ND; Mark and Shelley Hollis; Mike Jollon; Jean Keene, "the Eagle Lady"; the Kircher family; Bill and Jeannie Konz; Debbie and Marie Konz; Steve and Garret Kroschel; Benny and Stephanie Langholt; Jason and Judy Levi; Janet Lynch; Mark and Karen McVery; Alex Mercer; Sherrie and Mike Miller; Steve Oomituk; Carla Pagi; Todd and Jen Parker; Jack and Janet Rose; Howard Schargel; Scott and Heidi Schoppenhorst; Andy Scott; Tony and Denise Shafer; Ben and Gretchen Shaw; Dennis, Alane, Joe, and

LEFT *A male and female polar bear on the pack ice*

Anna Simmons; Robert Simpson; Paul Splan; Kevin Stewart; Nathan Sutton; Steve and Rena Tarola; Tom Tincher; Leith Van Diemen; Steve White; Louis Zucchi; and many others. They have always shined a little light on the darkest and loneliest of days.

Finally, to all the unnamed people who have always lent a hand—whether a meal, a free tire, or a host of other essentials that make this type of lifestyle possible—I thank you.

From Theodore Roosevelt IV

Over the years, I have been extremely lucky to work with some of the best minds thinking about climate change. The staff at the Pew Center ably led by Eileen Claussen had the patience to educate me on the topic while acting as a bridge between American business leaders and policy makers in Washington DC. World Resources Institute under the imaginative direction of Jonathan Lash created coalitions where none existed and deserves much credit for helping me see the economic opportunities arising from policies addressing climate change. My brilliant colleague at Lehman Brothers, John Llewellyn, wrote a report, *The Business of Climate Change,* that is the best of its kind. On my trips to Alaska, organizations there—Trustees for Alaska, Alaska Conservation Solutions, and the Wilderness Society—went to extraordinary lengths to allow me to see firsthand the impact of climate change on that beautiful yet fragile land. All of them made an investment in me that I will never be able to repay.

From Richard Nelson

I am profoundly grateful to the Iñupiaq people of Wainwright, Alaska, for their kindness, hospitality, and teachings—which completely changed the course of my life. My special thanks to Steven Kazlowski, not only for making my visit to the Beaufort Sea coast possible, but for adding such companionable pleasure to days as remarkable as any I've ever experienced. Finally, my sincere thanks to Steven Amstrup

and Geoffrey York for reading, correcting, and augmenting the information on polar bear biology in my essay.

From Nick Jans

I wish to express my deep gratitude to the following North Slope residents who were more than generous with their time and knowledge and extended their hospitality to a stranger: Johnny Lee Aiken, Gordon Brower, Geoff Carroll, Richard Glenn, Craig George, Mayor Edward Itta, Shanna Johnson, Leonard Lampe, and John Luhrs. Thanks also to Daren Beaudo of BP and Luci Beach of the Gwich'in Steering Committee. To those whom I've forgotten to mention, forgive me. Finally, I wish to offer humble thanks to Sarah Kunaqnana of Nuiqsut, who remembers another time, and whose generosity of spirit should inspire us all. *Aarigaa, taiku.*

Scientific Consultants

The publisher wishes to thank U.S. Geological Survey biologists Steven K. Amstrup, Geoffrey S. York, and Anthony S. Fischbach for their assistance in reviewing the scientific information in *The Last Polar Bear,* as well as for their ongoing work in Arctic Alaska on behalf of the polar bear and other Arctic creatures. Amstrup, the leading polar bear biologist of the U.S. Geological Survey, based at the Alaska Science Center in Anchorage, has been conducting research on all aspects of polar bear ecology in the Beaufort Sea for nearly twenty-five years. York, a colleague of Amstrup's on the Polar Bear Project, has been a USGS biologist at the Alaska Science Center since 1995. Fischbach is a wildlife biologist for the USGS in the Walrus Research Program at the Alaska Science Center.

Environmental Sponsors

Braided River Books gratefully acknowledges the support of the following organizations in the production of this book and corresponding public outreach.

Alaska Wilderness League leads the effort to preserve Alaska's wilderness by engaging citizens, sharing resources, collaborating with other organizations, educating the public, and providing a courageous, constant, and victorious voice for Alaska in the nation's capital. Please visit *www.AlaskaWild.org* for up-to-date information on impacts to the polar bear and its Arctic habitat.

Legal action by the **Natural Resources Defense Council** helped spark a global outcry over the plight of the polar bear and forced the Bush administration to propose protecting the bear under the Endangered Species Act. Backed by 1.2 million members and online activists, NRDC is now mobilizing the American public in support of strong measures to reduce global-warming pollution, move America beyond oil dependence, and slow the melting of the polar bear's Arctic sea ice habitat. For more information, visit *www.PolarBearSOS. org* and *www.nrdc.org*.

For more information on booking a multimedia event based upon *The Last Polar Bear,* please inquire at info@BraidedRiverBooks.org.

Traveling Exhibit

An exhibit based on the book *The Last Polar Bear* features the work of Steven Kazlowski and was created by the **Burke Museum of Natural History and Culture** in collaboration with the publisher, Braided River Books. The exhibit includes additional images that do not appear in the publication. The Burke Museum was founded in 1885 and has been located on the University of Washington campus in Seattle throughout its history. The Burke is the premier museum of natural history and culture in the Pacific Northwest, presenting exhibitions, producing public education programs, and caring for collections that reflect the region's natural and cultural diversity. In 2007 it launched a national traveling exhibition program, partnering with Braided River Books on several wildlife conservation exhibits. "The Last Polar Bear" is the second of these exhibitions to travel.

Left Eye Productions is dedicated to producing top-quality nature and wildlife images that give the general public, who will never see most of these places or things, a sense of what could be lost. For information, visit *www.lefteyepro.com*.

Suggested Reading

Alaska Department of Fish and Game. "Subsistence Land Use in Upper Yukon-Porcupine Communities, Alaska." By Richard A. Caulfield for Division of Subsistence. Technical Paper No. 16. Fairbanks, AK, 1983.

Alley, Richard B. *The Two-Mile Time Machine: Ice Cores, Abrupt Climate Change, and Our Future.* Princeton, NJ: Princeton University Press, 2002.

Amstrup, Steven C., and C. Gardner. "Polar Bear Maternity Denning in the Beaufort Sea." *Journal of Wildlife Management* 58 (1994):1–10.

Anderson, Will. *Green Up!* Devon, England: Green Books, 2007.

Arctic Climate Impact Assessment Group. *Arctic Climate Impact Assessment.* New York: Cambridge University Press, 2005, *www.acia.uaf.edu/pages/scientific.html.*

Balish, Chris. *How to Live Well Without Owning a Car.* Berkeley, CA: Ten Speed Press, 2006.

Banerjee, Subhankar. *Arctic National Wildlife Refuge: Seasons of Life and Land.* Seattle: The Mountaineers Books, 2003.

Braasch, Gary. *Earth Under Fire: How Global Warming Is Changing the World.* Berkeley, CA: University of California Press, 2007.

Brown, Lester R. *Plan B 2.0: Rescuing a Planet Under Stress and a Civilization in Trouble.* New York: W. W. Norton, 2006.

Brown, Stephen, ed. *Arctic Wings: Birds of the Arctic National Wildlife Refuge.* Seattle: The Mountaineers Books, 2006.

Bruemmer, Fred. *Polar Dance: Born of the North Wind.* Photographs by Thomas D. Mangelsen. Edited by Cara Blessley. Park City, UT: Images of Nature Gallery, 1997.

Calef, George. *Caribou and the Barren-Lands.* Ottawa, ON: Firefly Books Ltd. with Canadian Arctic Resources Committee, 1981.

Cogwell, Mathew T. *Arctic National Wildlife Refuge.* Hauppauge, NY: Nova Science Publishers, 2002.

Collins, George, and Lowell Sumner. "The Northeast Arctic: The Last Great Wilderness." *Sierra Club Bulletin* 13 (October 1953):12–26.

Cone, Marla. *Silent Snow: The Slow Poisoning of the Arctic.* New York: Grove Press, 2005.

Craighead, Charlie, and Bonnie Kreps. *Arctic Dance: The Mardy Murie Story.* Portland, OR: Graphic Arts Center Publishing, 2002.

Dabcovich, Lydia. *The Polar Bear Son: An Inuit Tale.* New York: Clarion Books, 1999.

Dauncey, Guy, and Patrick Mazza. *Stormy Weather: 101 Solutions to Global Climate Change.* Gabriola Island, BC: New Society Publishers, 2001.

David, Laurie. *Stop Global Warming: The Solution Is You!* Golden, CO: Fulcrum Publishing, 2006.

Dessler, Andrew E., and Edward A. Parson. *The Science and Politics of Global Climate Change: A Guide to the Debate.* New York: Cambridge University Press, 2006.

Diamond, Jared. Collapse: *How Societies Choose to Fare or Succeed.* New York: Penguin Books, 2005.

Dotto, Lydia. *Storm Warning: Gambling with the Climate of Our Planet.* Toronto: Doubleday Canada, 2000.

Dow, Kim, and Thomas E. Downing. *The Atlas of Climate Change: Mapping the World's Greatest Challenge.* Berkeley, CA: University of California Press, 2006.

E Magazine. *Green Living: The E Magazine Handbook for Living Lightly on the Earth.* New York: Plume, 2005.

Fancy, Steven G., and Kenneth R. Whitten. "Selection of Calving Sites by Porcupine Herd Caribou." *Canadian Journal of Zoology* 69 (1991):1736–1743.

Flannery, Tim. *The Weather Makers: How Man Is Changing the Climate and What It Means for Life on Earth.* New York: Atlantic Monthly Press, 2006.

Gelbspan, Ross. *Boiling Point: How Politicians, Big Oil and Coal, Journalists, and Activists Are Fueling the Climate Crisis–And What We Can Do to Avert Disaster.* New York: Basic Books, 2004.

George, Jean Craighead. *Snow Bear.* New York: Hyperion, 2003.

Glick, Daniel. "GeoSigns: The Big Thaw." *National Geographic Magazine,* September 2004, *http://magma.nationalgeographic.com/ngm/0409/feature2/fulltext.html.*

Gore, Al. *An Inconvenient Truth: The Crisis of Global Warming.* New York: Viking Juvenile, 2007.

——. *An Inconvenient Truth: The Planetary Emergency of Global Warming and What We Can Do About It.* Emmaus, PA: Rodale Books, 2006.

Grist Magazine. *Wake Up and Smell the Planet: The Non-Pompous, Non-Preachy Grist Guide to Greening Your Day.* Seattle: The Mountaineers Books, 2007.

Hartmann, Thom. *The Last Hours of Ancient Sunlight: The Fate of the World and What We Can Do Before It's Too Late.* New York: Three Rivers Press, 2004.

Henson, Robert. *The Rough Guide to Climate Change.* London: Rough Guides, 2006.

Hess, Bill. *Gift of the Whale: The Iñupiat Bowhead Hunt, a Sacred Tradition.* Seattle: Sasquatch Books, 2003.

Intergovernmental Panel on Climate Change. *Climate Change 2007: Impacts, Adaptation, and Vulnerability.* New York: Cambridge University Press, 2007.

Jans, Nick. *The Last Light Breaking: Living Among Alaska's Iñupiat Eskimos.* Portland, OR: Graphic Arts Center Publishing, 1994.

Jones, Ellis, Ross Haenfler, and Brett Johnson. *Better World Handbook: Small Changes That Make a Big Difference.* Gabriola Island, BC: New Society Publishers, 2007.

Kolbert, Elizabeth. *Field Notes from a Catastrophe: Man, Nature, and Climate Change.* New York: Bloomsburg USA, 2006.

Leakey, Richard. *The Sixth Extinction: Patterns of Live and the Future of Humankind.* New York: Anchor, 1996.

Lentfer, Hank, and Carolyn Servid, comps. *Arctic Refuge: A Circle of Testimony.* Minneapolis, MN: Milkweed Editions, 2001.

Linden, Eugene. *The Winds of Change: Climate, Weather, and the Destruction of Civilizations.* New York: Simon and Schuster, 2006.

Lockwood, Sophie. *Polar Bears.* Mankato, MN: The Child's World, 2005.

Lopez, Barry. *Arctic Dreams: Imagination and Desire in a Northern Landscape.* New York: Vintage, 2001.

Lovelock, James. *The Revenge of Gaia: Earth's Climate Crisis and the Fate of Humanity.* New York: Perseus Books Group, 2007.

Madsen, Ken, and Norma Kassi. *Under the Arctic Sun: Gwich'in, Caribou, and the Arctic National Wildlife Refuge.* Englewood, CO: Westcliffe Publishers, 2002.

McKibben, Bill. *The End of Nature.* New York: Random House, 2006.

Miller, Debbie S. *Midnight Wilderness: Journeys in Alaska's Arctic National Wildlife Refuge.* Portland, OR: Alaska Northwest Books, 2002.

Miller, Debbie S., with illustrations by Jon Van Zyle. *A Polar Bear Journey.* New York: Walker Books for Young Readers, 2005.

Monbiot, George, and Dr. Matthew Prescott. *Heat: How to Stop the Planet from Burning.* Cambridge, MA: South End Press, 2007.

Motavalli, Jim, ed. *Feeling the Heat: Dispatches from the Front Lines of Climate Change.* London: Routledge, 2004.

Murie, Margaret. E. *Two in the Far North.* Portland, OR: Alaska Northwest Books, 1997.

National Research Council. *Cumulative Environmental Effects of Oil and Gas Activities on Alaska's North Slope.* Washington DC: The National Academies Press, 2003.

Nelson, Richard. *Hunters of the Northern Ice.* Chicago: University of Chicago Press, 1972.

Ovsyanikov, Nikita. *Polar Bears: Living with the White Bear.* Osceola, WI: Voyageur Press, 1998.

Pearce, Fred. *With Speed and Violence: Why Scientists Fear Tipping Points in Climate Change.* Boston, MA: Beacon Press, 2007.

Penny, Malcolm. *Polar Bear: Habitats, Life Cycles, Food Chains, Threats.* Orlando, FL: Raintree Steck-Vaughn Publishers, 2000.

Peter, Katherine. *Neetsaii Gwiindaii: Living in the Chandalar Country.* Fairbanks: University of Alaska Fairbanks, Alaska Native Language Center, 1992.

Philander, S. George. *Is the Temperature Rising? The Uncertain Science of Global Warming.* Princeton, NJ: Princeton University Press, 2000.

Pielou, E. C. *A Naturalist's Guide to the Arctic.* Chicago: University of Chicago Press, 1994.

Quammen, David. *Monster of God: The Man-Eating Predator in the Jungles of History and the Mind.* New York: Norton, 2003.

Rennick, Penny, ed. *Arctic National Wildlife Refuge.* Anchorage: Alaska Geographic Society, 1993.

Romm, Joseph. *Hell and High Water: Global Warming—the Solution and the Politics—and What We Should Do.* New York: William Morrow, 2006.

Rosing, Norbert. *The World of the Polar Bear.* Richmond Hill, ON: Firefly Books, 2006.

Ruddiman, William F. Plows, *Plagues, and Petroleum: How Humans Took Control of Climate.* Princeton, NJ: Princeton University Press, 2005.

Schneider, Stephen H., and Terry Root, eds. *Wildlife Responses to Climate Change: North American Case Studies.* Washington DC: Island Press, 2001.

Schneider, Stephen H., Armin Rosencranz, and John O. Niles, eds. *Change Policy: A Survey.* Washington DC: Island Press, 2002.

Sherwonit, Bill, and Tom Walker. *Alaska's Bears: Grizzlies, Black Bears, and Polar Bears.* Portland, OR: Alaska Northwest Books, 1998.

Sloman, Lynn. *Car Sick: Solutions for Our Car-Addicted Culture.* Devon, England: Green Books, 2006.

Smith, Thomas S., Steven Herrero, and Terry D. DeBruyn. "Alaskan Brown Bears, Humans, and Habituation." *Ursus* 16 (2005):1–10.

Speth, James Gustave. *Red Sky at Morning: America and the Crisis of the Global Environment.* 2nd ed. New Haven, CT: Yale University Press, 2005.

Steffen, Alex. *Worldchanging: A User's Guide for the 21st Century.* New York: Henry N. Abrams, 2006.

Stirling, Ian. *Polar Bears.* Ann Arbor: University of Michigan Press, 1999.

Truett, Joe C., and Stephen R. Johnson, eds. *The Natural History of an Arctic Oil Field.* San Diego, CA: Academic Press, 2000.

U.S. Department of Agriculture, Forest Service. *The Arctic National Wildlife Refuge: An Exploration of the Meanings Embodied in America's Last Great Wilderness.* By Roger Kaye. Rocky Mountain Research Station Proceeding RMRS-P-15, vol. 2 (2000):73–80.

U.S. Department of the Interior, Fish and Wildlife Service, Northern Ecological Services. Kaktovik Subsistence: *Land Use Values through Time in the Arctic National Wildlife Refuge Area.* By Michael J. Jacobson and Cynthia Wentworth. Fairbanks, AK, 1982.

U.S. Department of the Interior, Fish and Wildlife Service. *Final Report–Baseline Study of the Fish, Wildlife, and Their Habitats, Arctic National Wildlife Refuge Coastal Plain Resource.* By G. W. Garner and P. E. Reynolds. Anchorage, AK, 1986.

U.S. Department of the Interior, Fish and Wildlife Service. *Effects of Prudhoe Bay Reserve Pit Fluids on Water Quality and Microinvertebrates of Arctic Tundra Ponds in Alaska.* By Robin L. West and Elaine Snyder-Conn. Biological Report 7. Washington DC, 1987.

U.S. Geological Survey, Biological Resources Division. *Arctic Refuge Coastal Plain Terrestrial Wildlife Research Summaries.* Edited by D. C. Douglas, P. E. Reynolds, and E. B. Rhode. Biological Science Report USGS/BRD/ BSR-2002-0001. Washington DC, 2002.

Ward, Kennan. *Journeys with the Ice Bear.* Minnetonka, MN: Northword Press, 1996.

——. *The Last Wilderness: Arctic National Wildlife Refuge.* Santa Cruz, CA: WildLight Press, 2001.

Watkins, Tom H., et al. *Vanishing Arctic: Alaska's National Wildlife Refuge.* New York: Aperture, 1988.

Weller, Gunter, and Patricia A. Anderson, eds. *Assessing the Consequences of Climate Change for Alaska and the Bering Sea Region.* Workshop proceedings, Center for Global Change and Arctic System Research, University of Alaska–Fairbanks, Fairbanks, November 1999:1–94.

Whitten, Kenneth R., and Raymond D. Cameron. "Distribution of Caribou Calving in Relation to the Prudhoe Bay Oilfield." In *The Proceedings of the First North American Caribou Workshop,* Whitehorse, Yukon, edited by Art M. Martell and Don E. Russell, 33–39. Ottawa, ON: Canadian Wildlife Service, 1985.

Wohlforth, Charles. *The Whale and the Supercomputer: On the Northern Front of Climate Change.* New York: North Point Press, 2005.

ABOVE *Arctic tern*

Index

Braided River Books—a conservation imprint of **The Mountaineers Books**—combines photography and writing to bring a fresh perspective to key environmental issues facing western North America's wildest places. Our books reach beyond the printed page as we take these distinctive voices and visions to a wider audience through lectures, exhibits, and multimedia events. Our goal is to inspire and motivate people to support critical conservation efforts and make a definitive difference. Please visit www.BraidedRiverBooks.org for more information on events, exhibits, speakers, and how to contribute to support this work.

Braided River books may be purchased for corporate, educational, or other promotional sales. For special discounts and information, contact our sales department at 1-800-553-4453 or mbooks@mountaineersbooks.org.

The Mountaineers, founded in 1906, is a nonprofit outdoor activity and conservation club whose mission is "to explore, study, preserve, and enjoy the natural beauty of the outdoors…" **The Mountaineers Books** supports the club's mission by publishing travel and natural history guides, instructional texts, and works on conservation and history. **The Mountaineers Foundation** is a public foundation established in 1968 to promote the study of the mountains, forests, and streams of the Pacific Northwest and to contribute to the preservation of its natural beauty and ecological integrity.

Send or call for our catalog of more than 500 outdoor titles:

The Mountaineers Books
1001 SW Klickitat Way, Suite 201
Seattle, WA 98134
800-553-4453
mbooks@mountaineersbooks.org
www.mountaineersbooks.org

BRAIDED RIVER
CHANGING PERSPECTIVES

1001 SW Klickitat Way, Suite 201
Seattle, WA 98134
www.BraidedRiverBooks.org

Manufactured in China

Project Manager: Kris Fulsaas
Acquisition Editors: Helen Cherullo, Deb Easter
Director of Editorial and Production: Kathleen Cubley
Left Eye Productions Project Manager: Sundra Coulson
Developmental Editors: Christine Clifton-Thornton, Deb Easter, Ingrid Emerick
Copy Editor: Julie Van Pelt
Educational Outreach Director: Kerry Smith
Cover design: Jane Jeszeck, Jigsaw/www.jigsawseattle.com
Book design and layout: Jane Jeszeck, Jigsaw
Map art and design: Rose Michelle Taverniti
Map relief: Dee Molenaar
Illustrator: Jennifer Shontz

All photographs by Steven Kazlowski except as noted. All images were taken in the Arctic, with the exception of some essayist portraits and the image on page 10.

COVER *A polar bear sow with cub traveling and hunting on multiyear ice (summer, Chukchi Sea)* / PAGE 1 *A cub plays with a piece of bowhead whale baleen.* / FRONTISPIECE *A polar bear sow and cub in the midnight sun (coastal plain, Arctic National Wildlife Refuge)* / TITLE PAGE *Aurora borealis (southern foothills of the Brooks Range, Arctic National Wildlife Refuge)* / PAGE 4 *A polar bear emerges from the sea as Arctic terns wheel above (Arctic coast, Arctic National Wildlife Refuge).* / BACK COVER *A young polar bear (coastal plain, Arctic National Wildlife Refuge)*

Library of Congress Cataloging-in-Publication Data

Kazlowski, Steven.
  The last polar bear / Steven Kazlowski. -- 1st ed.
    p. cm.
  Includes bibliographical references and index.
  ISBN 978-1-59485-059-2 (hb)
  1. Polar bear--Climatic factors. 2. Polar bear--Pictorial works. I.
Title.
QL737.C27K39 2008
599.786--dc22
                                2007035265